Good

to

Eat

Good
to
Eat

Real food to nourish and sustain you for life

David Atherton

HODDER &
STOUGHTON

Contents

From left to right: Slaw is raw salad topped with Falafel bites (see page 125), Quick bean squashy chilli (see page 161), Bánh xèo (see page 152) with Sourdough loaf (see page 27).

Introduction

I love to eat. I love experiencing different flavours, textures and aromas. But I also love the culture and artistry of food. The stories we tell through food. The beauty of a neat slice of cake...

And, I'll admit it, I love the science of food. Perhaps it's because of my job as a health professional, but the science behind nutrition fascinates me. Nutrition is where food, health and exercise — three of my passions — collide. There's a lot of science behind baking, too, which is perhaps partly what drew me to it in the first place. Well, that and the cake, of course.

Why 'good to eat'?

I grew up vegetarian, but at the age of 18 I started eating meat. For I while, I went completely the other way and ate anything and everything — mice, rat, duck embryos, snake, goat testicles, you name it. Nowadays, I don't slap any particular label on my diet. Fish features occasionally, but I haven't eaten meat for years. (My days of eating goat testicles are long gone.) The overwhelming bulk of my food now comes from plants — fruits, vegetables and whole grains.

Like many people, I've gone through evangelically healthy periods in my life. Periods where I've researched and thought carefully about the nutritional value of the foods I eat, for my health, and sometimes because I've wanted to change the way my body looks. For a lot of my friends, eating healthily has simply meant restricting the amount of food they eat and reducing calories, but that's never sat well with me. Faddy or strict diets don't work for me because I hate following a set of food 'rules' like it's a religion, and I think your diet should be sustainable in the long term. I just want food that's good for me, and plenty of it.

The turning point came a few years ago when I got seriously into cycling and fitness. I've always been an active person, but I realised that I needed to eat intelligently to fuel my body. And while I don't eat lots of sugar and fat, I had to increase the amount of food I consumed, so I thought more carefully about when I was eating. I realised that eating healthily does not have to mean depriving myself of tasty, filling food.

This realisation coincided with increasing research on the microbiome – the trillions of bacteria, fungi and other microbes that live on and in the human body, especially in the gut. We're learning more and more about the microbiome and its importance to all areas of health, all the time. You can buy prebiotics to feed your friendly gut bacteria, and probiotics that add to them, but the best way to improve the diversity of good micro-organisms in your gut is to eat loads of fruit, veg, whole grains and fermented foods. That's how I eat and it's at the heart of this book. In other words, this book feeds you and all your bacterial friends.

It's been an interesting journey discovering the foods that are good for me and good to eat. I now enjoy my exercise more, I'm much more efficient in my exercise, I maintain a healthy weight without fuss, and I love what I'm eating. I love my food not just because it's good for me, but also because it tastes great.

So when I made it onto the tenth season of *The Great British Bake Off*, I was determined to stick to my own style of cooking, one that makes dishes healthier where possible, by substituting sugar and fat for grated root veg and so on. I'm a firm believer that healthier food doesn't have to mean tasteless food, and if I can substitute a few hundred grams of sugar here, a packet of butter there, and still win a national baking competition, it must be true!

In my kitchen

For all the current focus on speedy food, speed isn't always best. Sure, it's good to have some quick recipes under your belt – and you'll find plenty in this book – but good food is about the whole process, not just quick results. It's about having fun and being in the moment. In this way, good food can be meditative, and it's okay if it sometimes takes an hour or two – or, in the case of sourdoughs and fermented foods – days or even weeks.

This is my way of saying that I don't have a lot of kit and gimmicky gadgets in my kitchen designed to speed up processes. I like to touch the food I'm cooking. I much prefer kneading bread by hand, for example, than letting a stand mixer do the hard work for me. Besides, I like to get my hands dirty.

So rather than having drawers stuffed with items that I only use once a year, I have a few really good pieces of equipment that I use all the time:

- **Digital scales** – *a must for any baker. You can't always 'eyeball' amounts in baking.*

- **Spatula** – *a really good spatula is a wonderful thing. I like the type that can withstand high heat and slides round a bowl to leave it looking like it's been washed clean.*

- **Microplane grater** – *great for mincing garlic and ginger, but also for all kinds of grating.*

- **Flour brush** – *brilliant for gently brushing flour off your bakes . . . and your work surface. (If you use a wet cloth, you end up creating a gluey paste that's so hard to remove.)*

- **Knife-sharpening steel** – *you don't need very fancy knives, but you do need to keep them sharp. Properly sharp knives make chopping, slicing and paring an absolute dream.*

- **Thermapen digital thermometer** – *this one's a bit of a splurge item (saying that, I stole mine from the* Bake Off *tent!), but it's extremely useful for measuring temperatures accurately.*

- **Jars** – *great for storing spices, pickling veg, fermenting foods and simply shaking up a quick dressing. You can never have too many jars, and I save almost every one that comes my way.*

There are also certain ingredients that I always have handy at home. These are what I call my 'hero ingredients' – ingredients that pack a huge nutritional punch, that are sorely undervalued, or that add maximum flavour to healthy dishes without loading up on the sugar and fat. You'll find these hero ingredients highlighted throughout the book, and I strongly recommend you start building up your own stash.

Speaking of stashes, every two months or so I make up a massive jar (seriously, a huge jar) of mixed nuts, seeds and dried fruit, which I use to top porridge, desserts, smoothie bowls, etc. This gives an easy daily boost of fibre, nutrients and indigestible starches to feed your microbiome. Try making up your own mix with whatever nuts, seeds and dried fruit you like. I add cacao nibs, too, for a cheeky chocolatey hit.

In this book

I may be known for healthy bakes but this book contains proper meals as well as baking recipes. It's structured around the way I cook and eat, and contains the recipes that I turn to time and time again.

There are breakfast and lunch ideas, delicious mix-and-match salads, meals for midweek eating, dishes to impress your friends, bread to bake when you need to slow life down, tasty treats to take into the office or on a bike ride, as well as special-occasion cakes and everyday puddings.

All are simple to make (I don't know about you, but I've got a busy life and a fairly average-sized London kitchen). Most are really inexpensive (using fresh ingredients and cooking from scratch saves me a fortune). And all are designed to nourish and sustain you (without a side order of guilt).

That, then, is the goal of this book: to show how food can be delicious, moreish, comforting and good for you. I know this because the recipes included are the foods I eat all the time. I eat real bread. I tuck into satisfying meals after work. I bake cakes and biscuits. And so should you. When it's part of a balanced lifestyle, why shouldn't you enjoy your food?

The recipes in this book aren't written with health fanatics in mind – although they'll work brilliantly around exercise if that's your thing (think healthy pasta bakes for carb loading, energy balls for that pre-workout boost and nutritious food to throw in the oven when you're ravenous after a run). They're designed for anyone who loves their food, or wants to love their food but isn't prepared to sacrifice their waistline and long-term health in the process. You can therefore use this book to support a more active lifestyle – or you can simply enjoy an evening meal and slice of cake that are better for you . . .

Bread is back

sourdough made easy

Sourdough made simple

Sourdough bread wasn't always called sourdough bread. It used to be called, well, just bread. Before we came to use baker's yeast – which originated as a by-product of the brewing industry – all bread was sourdough. Imagine that? Long before sourdough ever became fashionable, even the most basic home-made loaf would have used wild yeasts, bacteria and a long ferment to produce that highly desirable chewy texture and complicated flavours. Then along came baker's yeast – which is quick, predictable and produces a consistent, soft crumb – and breadmaking was transformed. Thankfully, shoppers and home bakers are now rediscovering the delights of sourdough.

Why simple sourdough?

Sourdough is one of those things that's beautifully simple but involves a few stages. Even as a bread obsessive, someone who's been baking bread for years and read many books by bread experts, I'm often surprised at how intimidating instructions for making sourdough can be.

But they don't have to be, and making sourdough is something that everyone can do. That's why I've included a section on easy sourdough in this book. Written for total novices, this is my way of stripping back this loaf to its simplest process. Treat it as a basic sourdough method to get you (if you'll excuse the pun) started. Once you've got the hang of it, feel free to experiment and get as technical and faffy as you want.

While the essence of sourdough might be simple, the health benefits are complex and we are still only getting glimpses of the mighty power of this simple food. In my day job as a health professional I speak to countless people who have irritable bowel syndrome (IBS), and the most common perceived cause of their ailment seems to be gluten. I'm always a little confused when they declare that they can't eat gluten, but they can eat sourdough. Sourdough made with wheat flour has the same amount of gliadin (the gluten protein in wheat that usually causes problems) as regular bread. If it isn't the gluten in the bread that is causing the problems, what is it? One answer lies in the long ferment of sourdough. The fermentation process essentially pre-digests the flour and reduces phytic acid (responsible for digestive discomfort and bloating). Phytic acid also binds to key nutrients that stop us from absorbing them, so reducing this increases the bioavailability of key nutrients. Wholegrain flours feed your gut bacteria with indigestible starches (prebiotics) and a healthy gut produces all kinds of short-chain fatty acids that support good health from your gut through to your mind, and can even control blood pressure, weight and your blood sugar.

Okay, enough of the science; basically, sourdough bread is good for you, a home-made loaf can cost as little as 30p, and takes just 20 minutes of your time (spread out over about 24 hours).

It's all about the journey

When you make a cake, providing you follow the measurements and instructions exactly, you'll get the result you expect. Sourdough is much more experiential than that; you have to get a feel for it. You have to get to know your starter, your equipment, your oven and your flour over time. Sure, you may nail it with your first loaf (probably not, if my experience is anything to go by), but even if you do, you're bound to come unstuck and have failures at some point. Practice makes perfect, as they say. This is all part of the process and, if we're honest, the allure of sourdough. This is not quick, cookie-cutter baking but a slow, therapeutic process that is so rewarding.

But what is it that makes sourdough more complex than your ordinary loaf? After all, it's essentially just flour, salt and water. What contributes to this being a more involved process and creates the sourdough magic are micro-organisms – the lactobacilli bacteria (like those found in yogurt) and wild yeasts that live naturally on the flour. (If that sounds a bit gross, remember that, no matter how clean we are, our body is covered in bacterial cells. Yeasts and bacteria are everywhere. We may as well use them!)

Before we get into making the starter, there is myriad equipment available that sourdough bakers swear by that's worth investing in, and some that's not . . .

What kit do you really need?

In theory, getting started requires nothing but flour, salt and water, but you'll soon notice there's an abundance of fancy (and expensive) equipment aimed at sourdough bakers. You can buy these if you are really keen, but most of it is unnecessary. Here is the basic equipment I use; these items will help you get the best results – and maximum enjoyment – from your sourdough baking efforts.

Absolutely necessary:

- **Dough scraper** – *a very simple tool for easy breadmaking. It helps you to move the dough around while scraping, lifting and shaping it.*

- **Lame** – *essentially a razor blade on a handle a lame is vital to get a perfect slash in your bread dough. Because the blade is so sharp and thin you can get a quick cut without knocking any air out of the dough, which allows the dough to expand when cooking without splitting.*

- **Water spray bottle** – *to add moisture to the oven (see page 19 – or use water/ ice cubes) or to keep a loaf moist.*

- **Flour** – *I like to use VERY strong white bread flour for sourdough. Strong white bread flour works well, but if you can get the very strong stuff, try it out.*

Necessary if you want to make free-form loaves:

- **Baking stone** *(or, like me, you could use unglazed quarry tiles on a baking sheet, see page 19).*

- **Bannetons (proving baskets)** – *these give shape to a loaf. Sourdough loaves take time to prove and the basket provides support while the loaf slowly rises and builds structure. The best ones are made from natural fibres that manage humidity through the proving process, and which allow the loaf to be easily released when ready to bake.*

- **Bread cloche (or big cast-iron pot with a lid)** – *provides the perfect environment in which to bake bread. Steam released from the loaf when baking stays within the cloche, creating a humid environment, allowing the crust to remain supple and to stretch while rising.*

Optional extras, for the baker who likes to have all the right 'gear':

- **Bread peel** – *flat implement designed to easily and quickly slide your turned-out loaf into the oven. You can use a strong baking tray or a thin piece of wood.*

- **Flour brush** – *I love my flour brush, both for gently brushing excess flour off the uncooked loaf (without knocking any air out), and for cleaning up the work surface after kneading.*

- **Silicone loaf tin liner** – *I've used mine hundreds of times; it avoids you having to use baking paper to line tins.*

- **Beeswax cloth** – *to cover your dough instead of using cling film.*

Give your starter the best start

Start by choosing a good-sized jar. It is best to use a jar that will take up to three times the quantity of your starter; e.g. my jar holds 150g (1¼ cups/5oz) of starter and is a 350ml (12fl oz) jar. It is important to use a non-reactive container (reactive metals can chemically interfere with the starter). I suggest using a glass jar so that you can see your starter, but you can also use ceramic or enamelled metal. You can use plastic, but the starter is acidic and over time this can corrode the surface. It is best to use a non-reactive implement to mix the starter, too, but if you use stainless-steel, keep contact to a minimum.

Once I've started using my starter, I keep it in the fridge and take it out once a week to either use it to make bread, or to discard half (I use this to make pancakes or crackers – see pages 46 and 79), then I feed it with equal proportions of flour and water. When initially making the starter you want to keep it out of the fridge, as warmth will allow the micro-organisms to thrive. It is best to keep your jar at room temperature (about 26°C/80°F) and feed it with flour and water that is at least room temperature.

Lid on or lid off? It is important to cover your starter, but you don't have to tightly fit the lid (although I prefer to do this). You do not want your starter to dry out and get a crusty layer, and you do not want anything to fall into it. You can loosely place the lid on top if you feel safer doing this.

Do not worry if you see an explosion of activity at first, then your starter appears to be flat – it has not died. At the start there are different bacteria present that usually cause an explosion of bubbling, but these are not the bacteria you want for a successful starter. Eventually the lactic acid bacteria will dominate and your starter will become more acidic, killing off the other bacteria.

Remember, keep it warm and feed it regularly.

Getting your oven conditions right

Once your starter is nice and active, it's time to make your loaf. Once mixed, the next step to getting that perfect sourdough is all in the baking.

Bread is best baked in a humid environment, as this keeps the crust soft, so that it is better able to stretch and move as the loaf rises (this is especially important for the first 10–15 minutes once it hits the oven, as this is when it does most of its rising). Modern ovens use fans to remove moisture inside them for a crispier roast, so you'll have to take steps to put moisture back in. You can do this using a water spray, or by putting ice cubes or water into deep baking trays and setting them at the bottom of your oven. You can also use a bread cloche (either one specially made for the job or you can improvise with a cast-iron casserole pot), which traps moisture and creates a mini oven inside your oven.

Heat is also really important – you want your oven to be really hot for bread. To get a good rise you want the moisture in the bread to quickly evaporate, turning to steam, rising upwards and taking the dough with it. I find using an extra baking surface, such as a baking stone or old quarry tiles, means the bread bakes at a high temperature from the base and right through.

Top tips

When handling the dough I wet my hands first. This helps particularly when dealing with sticky doughs, because adding lots of flour will change its consistency.

Keeping your dough in a warm place to rise is important for the yeast to work optimally. It is best if the room temperature is about 26°C/80°F; if it is slightly cooler the dough will take longer to rise, and if it is hotter it will rise rapidly. In the winter I like to put my dough in a cold oven and add a bowl of just-boiled water. My mum used to put hers in the airing cupboard and some people even have a proving drawer. If I'm working from home I often put the bowl on my lap to prove, which gives me an even stronger connection to the bread.

Bread terms

Starter

Your starter is exactly what it says on the tin (or jar) – it is the start of your sourdough bread. It is an equal mixture of flour and water that has a colony of lactic-acid bacteria and yeasts fermenting the starches of the flour and giving it life. A starter requires feeding to remain active, I feed mine once a week as part of my breadmaking, but some people feed their starter every day.

Preferment

A preferment is a portion of your dough that is left to ferment before being added to the bulk of your flour, water and salt, and then kneaded. My preferment is equal parts flour and water, so is the same as my starter, and looks like a bubbly porridge. For the recipes in this book all the starter is added to the preferment, then a portion of the preferment is reserved as your starter before using the rest to make your dough. Preferment is a term used in non-sourdough recipes also and can include baker's yeast. It basically is a portion of your dough that is really active.

Stretch and fold

Stretch and fold is a simple action carried out through the proving period. You are essentially lifting a section of dough, stretching it away and then folding back down onto the dough. This stretches the gluten proteins (that like to be coiled) and improves the structure of your bread. It also helps regulate the temperature of the dough as a whole. This is a very quick and simple stage that will take 15 seconds, but it is vitally important to a good loaf.

Prove

Proving is a period where bread dough is allowed to rise. This is a time when you are not actively working with your dough, and the fermentation action of the yeast causes the dough to rise. Keeping your dough in a warm place speeds up the proving time, however this is not always required and sometimes you want to slow down the rise in a fridge. Most breads require a proving period prior to baking. If you have a long proving time, such as when baking sourdough, a banneton basket helps the dough to keep its shape.

Pre-shape

After your dough has finished proving in a bowl it will be bouncy and active. Pre-shaping sees you turn out your dough onto a surface and you do one last stretch and fold before leaving to relax ready for shaping.

Shape

There are lots of different techniques and tricks in shaping bread. Everyone finds their favourite way of doing it, but essentially you are looking to create tension across the dough so that it rises tall and proud with a good structure to the crumb. The same principles are used when doing fancy shapes.

Scoring

Because sourdough has a long ferment the outside of the dough becomes slightly tough (this will give you a good crust) and if you do not pre-score this before baking the bread will tear unpredictably as the loaf expands. Although we let our dough rise before baking, it still has a lot of rising to do in the oven and we want to control how this rise happens. A single score the length of the loaf will allow the dough to burst through in a uniform manner (hopefully). Scoring is achieved with a really thin sharp blade and most people use some form of a razor blade or lame (see page 17). This is definitely something that becomes easier with experience.

Simple sourdough starter

Making (or more correctly, growing) a sourdough starter is easier than you'd think. People get very worked up about how it should look and compare theirs to those pictured on the internet, but don't worry, no two starters are the same. Essentially, you are growing a cocktail of micro-organisms that are found naturally on flour. Remember that micro-organisms are EVERYWHERE and they just need some water and heat to get growing. Lots of starter recipes direct bakers to discard half the starter each day – this might seem wasteful, but this is simply to maximise the chance of getting a good range of yeasts and lactobacilli bacteria into the mix. My starter recipe tries to minimise the amount of discarded mix, and it always works for me.

This recipe makes 150g (1¼ cups/5oz) starter, which is the amount used for all the bread recipes in this book. I like to use my starter to make a preferment (mixing the starter with more flour and water and leaving it to go bubbly before combining it with the remaining ingredients to make a dough and keeping the remaining pre-ferment as the starter). This is a technique that means you do not have to faff around feeding your starter each day, and there is no waste.

Quantities for the recipes in this chapter:

Starter – 150g (1¼ cups/5oz)

Preferment – 450g (3¾ cups/1lb) (150g/1¼ cups/5oz starter mixed with 150g/ ⅔ cup/5oz water, 150g/1¼ cups/5oz flour)

Dough – 300g (2½ cups/10oz) of preferment is used to make the dough

Starter – 150g (1¼ cups/5oz) of preferment left is put back into a jar and becomes your starter for next time

Top tip 1 – Organic flours are best to use as non-organic flours may have residual chemicals designed to kill micro-organisms. Different grains will be colonised with different micro-organisms. In this recipe I use rye flour to increase the diversity of micro-organisms. Some people also add dried fruit such as raisins, or herbs such as basil, for the first two days to try to populate the starter with a diverse range of micro-organisms (these are then removed after two days).

Top tip 2 – If you want to give your starter the best chance possible, leave your water standing overnight before using it so that the chlorine evaporates.

Top tip 3 – If you would like to skip the whole starter stage, most sourdough bakeries will give you a small portion of their starter for free. If the bakery is using it, it must be good, and once you have used it a couple of times it will be your own. Once home, put 50g of starter into a jar with a lid, feed it with 50g (⅓ cup/2oz) strong white bread flour and 50g (¼ cup/2oz) warm water, then leave it for 24 hours. After that, it'll be ready to use in one of the bread recipes in this book.

Creating your starter

Organic strong white bread flour

Organic rye flour

Water (ideally water that has been left out on the counter overnight)

Day one: Put 25g (⅙ cup/scant 1oz) flour and 25g (⅛ cup/scant 1oz) warm water into a jar and mix well. Cover with a lid and leave in a warm place for 24 hours.

Day two: Add 15g (1 tbsp/½oz) rye flour, 10g (2 tsp/¼oz) bread flour and 25g (⅛ cup/scant 1oz) warm water to the jar and mix well. Cover with a lid and leave in a warm place for 24 hours.

Day three: Add 15g (1 tbsp/½oz) rye flour, 10g (2 tsp/¼oz) bread flour and 25g (⅛ cup/scant 1oz) warm water to the jar and mix. Cover with a lid and leave in a warm place for 24 hours.

If you check on your jar a few hours after feeding, hopefully you'll see activity already.

Day four: Remove 50g (⅓ cup/2oz) of the mix and discard, then add 25g (⅙ cup/scant 1oz) bread flour and 25g (⅛ cup/scant 1oz) warm water to the remaining starter. Mix well, cover with a lid, and leave in a warm place for 24 hours.

Day five: Remove 50g (⅓ cup/2oz) of the mix and discard, then add 25g (⅙ cup/scant 1oz) bread flour and 25g (⅛ cup/scant 1oz) warm water to the remaining starter. Mix well, cover with a lid, and leave in a warm place for 24 hours.

Day six: Your starter should be looking bubbly by now, so let's make some bread!

1. Active starter

2. Preferment

5. Shaping

6. Shaping

3. Stretch and fold

4. Flouring surface

7. Shaping

8. Shaping

This is my most basic free-form sourdough loaf. A free-form loaf is slightly trickier to make than a tin loaf, but this version is still very simple. Once again, the key to getting it right is experience and learning. As you get good at this loaf you can use different wholemeal flours or add all kinds of extras, such as nuts, seeds, dried fruit, grated root vegetables, herbs, cheeses, pickle liquors, wines, oils, malt extract, whole grains (amaranth works particularly well) or white miso – you are only constrained by your imagination.

150g (1¼ cups/5oz) sourdough starter (see page 23)

450g (3½ cups/1lb) strong white bread flour, plus extra for dusting

150g (1¼ cups/5oz) strong wholemeal (whole-wheat) bread flour

8g (1½ tsp) fine salt

Sourdough loaf

Stage 1 – Make your preferment.

Add the weighed-out 150g (1¼ cups/5oz) of your starter from the fridge into a bowl. Add 150g (1¼ cups/5oz) strong white bread flour and 150g (⅔ cup/5oz) warm water (35°C/95°F). Mix, cover and leave for 1 hour in a warm place.

Stage 2 – Make your dough.

Add 300g (2½ cups/10oz) of the preferment to a mixing bowl with the remaining 300g (2½ cups/10oz) strong white bread flour, the strong wholemeal bread flour, 230g (1 cup/8oz) warm water and the salt, and mix to a dough (you don't need to knead it to smooth, it will look quite rough). Cover and leave for 1 hour in a warm place. The remaining 150g (1¼ cups/5oz) of preferment can be put into a sealed jar in the fridge, as this is your starter ready for next time.

Stage 3 – Stretch and fold one.

Wet your hands and stretch and fold the dough inside the bowl. It is best to wet your hands at this stage to stop the dough sticking to your hands, but avoid adding lots of flour, as this will change the proportions of your dough. Slide your hand down the side of the dough, lifting it up (give it a wiggle to really stretch it out), then fold over to the other side of the bowl. Turn the bowl 90 degrees and repeat this process six times. Cover and leave for 1 hour in a warm place.

Stage 4 – Stretch and fold two.

Your dough should have started to rise now and will be more pillowy. Wet your hands and stretch and fold the dough inside the bowl, as before. Cover and leave for 1 hour in a warm place.

Stage 5 — Stretch and fold three.

Wet your hands and stretch and fold the dough inside the bowl as before. Cover and leave for 2 hours in a warm place.

Stage 6 — Pre-shape.

Tip your dough onto a lightly floured surface. Stretch and fold on the counter as before, then leave covered for 30 minutes.

Stage 7 — Shape.

Dust a banneton with flour. Shape the dough and place seam side up in the banneton. Leave on the counter for 30 minutes (until risen by at least 20% in volume), then place uncovered in the fridge overnight (about 10 hours).

Stage 8 — Bake.

Place a tray in the bottom of the oven containing at least 2cm (¾in) of boiling water.

Preheat the oven to 230°C fan (250°C/475°F/gas mark 9) with the baking stone (or heavy baking tray) already inside, if using. Remove your loaf from the fridge and leave it on the counter while the oven heats.

Once the oven is up to temperature, turn out your loaf onto a peel (or you can use a piece of stiff cardboard), brush off the flour, then score your loaf from the top to the bottom (about 1cm/½in deep), spray with water then slide onto the hot stone/tray in the oven.

Bake for 10 minutes, then reduce the heat to 200°C fan (220°C/425°F/gas mark 7) and bake for another 25 minutes.

Allow to cool completely before slicing, and store in a cotton bread bag at room temperature for up to three days. If you have any leftover, make into breadcrumbs or crackers.

N.B. if you are using a baking cloche, place in the oven to preheat, then bake for 30 minutes at 230°C fan (250°C/475°F/gas mark 9), before reducing the heat to 200°C fan (220°C/425°F/gas mark 7), removing the lid of the cloche, and baking for a further 10 minutes.

If you are new to sourdough this is the safest loaf to try. Also, a tin loaf is the most useful shape. I love a free-form sourdough loaf, but it's a lottery what size slice you're going to get. Understanding a sourdough schedule, finding your way with your starter and flour, and getting used to equipment can take time, but a tin makes all this a bit easier. I used to take my dough in a container on my bike to work and stretch and fold on my desk before shaping at home and baking the next morning. You will need one 20cm (8in) tin for this loaf.

150g (1¼ cups/5oz) sourdough starter (see page 23)

600g (5 cups/1lb 5oz) strong white bread flour, plus extra for dusting

8g (1½ tsp) fine salt

50g (2oz) mixed seeds (sesame, black sesame, chia seeds, hemp seeds, flaxseeds, poppy seeds, millet, whatever you choose. If you're using bigger seeds, such as pumpkin or sunflower, pulse them into smaller pieces in a food processor)

Seedy sourdough tin loaf

Stage 1 — Make your preferment.

Remove your starter from the fridge and weigh out 150g (1¼ cups/5oz). Add 150g (1¼ cups/5oz) of the flour and 150g (⅔ cup/5oz) warm water (35°C/95°F). Mix, cover and leave for 1 hour in a warm place.

Stage 2 — Make your dough.

Add 300g (2½ cups/10oz) of the preferment into your mixing bowl with the remaining 450g (3½ cups/1lb) flour, 230g (1 cup/8oz) warm water and the salt and mix to a dough (you don't need to knead it smooth, it will look quite rough). Cover and leave for 1 hour in a warm place. The remaining 150g (1¼ cups/5oz) of preferment can be put into a sealed jar in the fridge, as this is your starter ready for next time.

Stage 3 — Stretch and fold one.

Wet your hands and stretch and fold the dough inside the bowl (see page 27). Cover and leave for 1 hour in a warm place.

Stage 4 — Stretch and fold two.

Wet your hands and stretch and fold the dough inside the bowl, as before. Cover and leave for 1 hour in a warm place.

Stage 5 — Stretch and fold three.

Wet your hands and stretch and fold the dough inside the bowl, as before. Cover and leave for 2 hours in a warm place.

Stage 6 — Pre-shape.

Tip your dough onto a lightly floured surface. Stretch and fold the dough as before, then leave on the counter for 30 minutes.

Stage 7 – Shape.

Prepare your tin (use baking paper, or a tin liner if you have a galvanised tin, as sourdough really sticks). Prepare a plate with your seeds. Shape the dough, spray it with water (or wet your hand and rub it over the dough), leave for 1 minute for the dough to become tacky, then roll it in the seeds and place seam-side down in the tin. Leave on the counter until the dough just crests the top of the tin (usually about 30 minutes), then put it in the fridge overnight (at least 10 hours).

Stage 8 – Bake.

Place a tray in the bottom of the oven with at least 2cm (¾in) water.

Preheat the oven to 230°C fan (250°C/475°F/gas mark 9), remove your loaf from the fridge and leave it on the counter.

Once the oven is up to temperature, score the top of the loaf in a straight line down the middle, and spray it with water.

Bake for 10 minutes, then reduce the heat to 200°C fan (220°C/425°F/gas mark 7) and bake for another 20 minutes. Remove from the tin, return to the oven and bake for another 5–10 minutes (depending on how brown and crusty you want it). Allow to cool completely before slicing and store in a cotton breadbag at room temperature for up to three days. If you have any leftover, make into breadcrumbs or crackers.

Traditionally in towns across the UK, breweries and bakeries existed in a symbiosis. The breweries fermented grains and in the process created a foamy by-product (barm), that is full of yeasty goodness and was perfect for leavening bread. Eventually a yeast was isolated from this mixture, and this is what we use as baker's yeast today, but as a hark back to tradition this bread uses ale to boost a sourdough and give a lovely rich flavour to the crumb. Potato provides moistness and chew to the crumb, which for me is what sourdough bread is all about. Spelt is an ancient grain very closely related to wheat, which has a sweet and nutty flavour.

150g (1¼ cups/5oz) sourdough starter (see page 23)

500g (4 cups/1lb 2oz) strong white bread flour, plus extra for dusting

80g (⅔ cup/3½oz) spelt flour

20g (¾oz) ground flaxseeds

100ml (scant ½ cup/3fl oz) Yorkshire ale (other ales will suffice)

75g (3oz) finely grated potato

8g (1½ tsp) fine salt

Yorkshire ale sourdough loaf

Stage 1 – Make your preferment.

Remove your starter from the fridge and weigh out 150g (1¼ cups/5oz). Add 150g (1¼ cups/5oz) of the flour and 150g (⅔ cup/5oz) warm water (35°C/95°F). Mix, cover and leave for 1 hour in a warm place.

Stage 2 – Make your dough.

Add 300g (2½ cups/10oz) of the preferment to a mixing bowl with the rest of the strong white bread flour (350g/2¾ cups/12oz), spelt flour, ground flaxseeds, Yorkshire ale, 100g (scant ½ cup/3½oz) warm water, potato and salt and mix to a dough (you don't need to knead it smooth, it will look quite rough). Cover and leave for 1 hour in a warm place. The remaining 150g (1¼ cups/5oz) of preferment can be put into a sealed jar in the fridge, as this is your starter ready for next time.

Stage 3 – Stretch and fold one.

Wet your hands and stretch and fold the dough inside the bowl (see page 27). Cover and leave for 1 hour.

Stage 4 – Stretch and fold two.

Wet your hands and stretch and fold the dough inside the bowl. Cover and leave for 1 hour.

Stage 5 – Stretch and fold three.

Wet your hands and stretch and fold the dough inside the bowl. Cover and leave for 2 hours.

Stage 6 – Pre-shape.

Tip your dough onto a lightly floured surface. Stretch and fold it then leave on the counter for 45 minutes.

Stage 7 – Shape.

Dust a banneton with flour. Shape and then place the dough seam-side up in the banneton. Leave on the counter for 20 minutes (until risen by at least 20% in volume), then place in the fridge overnight (at least 10 hours).

Stage 8 – Bake.

Place a tray in the bottom of the oven containing at least 2cm (¾in) of boiling water.

Preheat the oven to 230°C fan (250°C/475°F/gas mark 9) with the baking stone (or heavy baking tray) already inside, if using. Remove your loaf from the fridge and leave it on the counter while the oven heats.

Once the oven is up to temperature, turn the loaf onto a peel (or you can use a piece of stiff cardboard), brush off the flour, then score the loaf as you please (about 1cm/½in deep), spray with water then slide onto the hot stone/tray in the oven.

Bake for 10 minutes, then reduce the heat to 200°C fan (220°C/425°F/gas mark 7) and bake for another 25 minutes. Allow to cool completely before slicing.

N.B. if you are using a baking cloche, place in the oven to preheat, then bake for 30 minutes at 230°C fan (250°C/475°F/gas mark 9), before reducing the heat to 200°C fan (220°C/425°F/gas mark 7), removing the lid of the cloche, and baking for a further 10 minutes.

Allow to cool completely before slicing and store in a cotton breadbag at room temperature for up to three days. If you have any leftover, make into breadcrumbs or crackers.

Wholemeal flour

I'm not going to bash white flour – I'm a baker, after all – but most of us know that wholemeal flours are better for us (more on why coming up). We also know that wholemeal flours change the taste and texture of bakes, which isn't necessarily desirable.

That's why, when a recipe calls for white flour, I often switch out a little of the white stuff for healthier wholemeal. The result? I still get the light and fluffy texture, but I know I'm giving my gut bacteria a feed. Not as much as when I'm eating 100% wholemeal, of course, but it's better than nothing, and I get to use my wholemeal flours for more than just brown bread.

Why we should all be using more wholemeal

Wholemeal flour includes the bran (outer husk) and germ (the embryo of the seed) of wheat grains. The bran and germ are where you find most of the nutrients and fibre, which is why wholemeal flour is more nutritious than white (which has had the bran removed).

Bread made with white flour contains a high amount of rapidly digestible starch, which has been linked to metabolic-related health problems, including diabetes. Whole grain wheat flours, on the other hand, contain a higher proportion of indigestible starch (known as resistant starch). These are called resistant because they resist digestion by the small intestine and instead move into the large intestine, where they slowly digest and ferment – providing prebiotics that feed our gut microbiome. This also makes us feel fuller for longer.

How to use this hero ingredient

Wholemeal flours provide lots of flavour and a heftier, denser texture, but that isn't always what you want. Sometimes you just want a light, fluffy bread or cake, and a purer taste.

There's some complex science around why wholemeal flour gives a heavier result. It's partly to do with glutathione and disulphide bonds – look this up if you enjoy geeking out. Essentially, there is something in wholemeal flour that blocks the gluten from bonding to each other and giving a lovely springy bread. Ascorbic acid (vitamin C) stops this happening, so you could always add some orange juice or a crushed vitamin C tablet to doughs that are high in wholemeal flour.

I've found that using a percentage of wholemeal in with white flour gives great results. So instead of using 100% white flour, add 5–10% of wholemeal and see how you go.

You'll find wholemeal flours in my:

- Sourdough loaf (see page 27)
- Morning baked bagels (see page 60)
- Beet burgers and sweet tato buns (see page 168)
- Saffron hot cross-less buns (see page 179)

Start as you mean to go on

breakfasts to keep you going all morning

For many of us, childhood breakfasts consisted of a piece of toast smeared with Marmite or a bowl of cereal – Rice Krispies or Coco Pops. I loved Weetabix, but I hated it when the biscuit shapes went soggy. It's interesting to see how so many people carry these types of breakfasts on into adulthood while, for the most part, our other eating habits evolve as we grow older.

I'm always amazed when I accidentally wander into the cereal aisle of a supermarket and see the sheer array of cereals that are clearly aimed, not at kids, but at adults – many of them marketed as healthy, slimming, fill-you-up-'til-lunch options. The wholesome choice for busy people on the go. The truth is, most of these cereals are highly processed, full of sugar, laden with salt, and they have you reaching for a snack within an hour. (They're also no quicker to serve up than a home-made, prepare-ahead breakfast.) And don't even get me started on the cereal bars, many of which are just chocolate bars dressed as muesli!

So if you're looking to build healthier habits, upgrading your breakfast is the ideal place to start. Literally, since you'll be starting your day as you mean to go on. Or even if you're not a cereal or toast junkie, if you already have your favourite everyday breakfast, this chapter will help you mix things up a bit, for when you fancy something different.

This chapter has speedy breakfast solutions such as overnight oats or granola, which are just about the quickest, tastiest, most nourishing breakfasts going (just a little prep in advance, then your mornings are sorted). Plus there are recipes for when you have more time on your hands, like my Sourdough sweet tato pancakes (page 46) or Blueberry muffins (page 52), which are perfect for a lazier weekend morning. All of them contain whole grains, nuts, seeds and fruit, so they're nutritious and filling. Real food to fuel your day. But, importantly, you're also starting your day with something special, not just shoving down food that's good for you but miserable to eat. That's no way to build lasting habits, believe me.

And if you're someone who routinely skips breakfast, you can eat these recipes at other times of the day. In fact, I encourage it. I often have porridge for lunch when I'm working from home. And who couldn't eat a blueberry muffin at 5 o'clock in the afternoon?

This is a speedy breakfast to prepare and is great if you have guests, but it is equally great as a breakfast staple to have at home or work. Baked oatmeal is like porridge cake in the US, where it is often served with cinnamon sugar and milk. It is usually very sweet and more of a cake than porridge, but this version is a lot more like baked porridge. It keeps very well and is still good three days after baking, especially if it is quickly warmed up and eaten with cold milk. I've made a frozen fruit yogurt for this recipe, but you can also throw the frozen fruit into the mix before baking, then serve with the yogurt.

250g (9oz) mixed
   frozen berries

150g (5oz) porridge oats
   (oatmeal)

100g (3½oz) rolled oats

1 tsp baking powder

2 tsp ground cinnamon

350ml (12fl oz)
   semi-skimmed milk

70g (2½oz) honey

40g (1½oz) ground flaxseeds

1 egg

1 banana, peeled

1 tsp vanilla extract

65g (2¼oz) walnut pieces

25g (1oz) caster
   (superfine) sugar

500g (1lb 2oz) Greek yogurt

Maple syrup, to serve

Nutty baked oatmeal

Remove the frozen fruit from the freezer. Preheat the oven to 180°C fan (200°C/400°F/gas mark 6). Line a 20cm x 20cm (8in x 8in) tin with baking parchment.

In a mixing bowl, toss together all the oats, the baking powder and cinnamon.

In a blender, whizz together the milk, honey, ground flaxseeds, egg, banana and vanilla until combined.

Pour the blender mixture into the dry ingredients in the mixing bowl and stir everything to combine. Transfer to the tin, then sprinkle over the walnuts and sugar. Bake in the oven for 30 minutes, then remove and cool on a wire rack, still in the tin.

Put the frozen fruit in a food processor and pulse a couple of times until the berries are broken up but still in big pieces. Remove two-thirds of them, then process the rest until smooth.

Put the Greek yogurt in a mixing bowl and stir with a spatula to loosen it slightly, then pour in the puréed fruit. Stir this through a couple of times so that it swirls through the yogurt. Add the rest of the fruit and stir a couple more times so that it too is swirled. You don't want to overmix.

When the baked oatmeal has cooled but is still warm, slice into 5cm (2in) squares in the tin, then lift out and stack with the fruity yogurt and serve with maple syrup.

Making your own yogurt is not difficult, is really cheap to do, and you get the benefits of a good dose of calcium and, most importantly, probiotic good bacteria to help your gut stay healthy. Essentially, the volume of yogurt you make is the same price as the volume of milk you use. Traditionally, yogurt has been made by inoculating milk with live lactic acid-producing bacterial cultures. It's a simple process, you add a small number of the bacteria to milk, then keep it warm and let them multiply. All yogurt used to be made like this, but most of the yogurt you now buy in the shop is milk that's been thickened, sweetened and is full of a whole host of additives (none of them being live bacteria). Making your own live yogurt couldn't be easier, it's just warm milk + starter yogurt + time. As with sourdough bread, you can get in deep with the science and all kinds of fancy equipment, but this simple recipe has always worked for me and is a great start. If you can get raw milk, or low pasteurised non-homogenised milk, this will give you the best yogurt, as it will retain lots of the natural array of bacteria and enzymes in these milks that are usually destroyed by pasteurisation.

500ml (16fl oz) whole milk

40g (1½oz) live yogurt (when you've made it once you can keep using your own yogurt, or use any good natural live bought yogurt)

Home-made yogurt

Put the milk in a saucepan and heat to 85°C (185°F). Remove from the heat and allow to cool to 45°C (113°F).

Stir in the yogurt, place a lid on top of the pan, then set somewhere insulated or warm overnight. Some people put it into their oven with just the oven light on, some place it in a Thermos or a specialised insulated yogurt container. I simply wrap my saucepan in a blanket and duvet and it has never failed me!

In the morning, whisk the yogurt until smooth. At this stage it will be a thin yogurt similar to a yogurt drink (which I love). If you want it thicker, secure a fine sieve over a bowl, line it with a fine muslin cloth or coffee filter and allow the yogurt to drain through until it reaches the desired consistency.

Just remember to save 40g (1½oz) of your yogurt to use as the starter for next time – pop it into a sealed container and store it in the fridge for up to 2 weeks.

Making your own granola is a great opportunity to use some of my hero ingredients (see page 10) or just some of your favourites, and adding different seeds, nuts, grains, fruits, oats and flours is a great way to feed your microbiome with a whole host of different prebiotics. Whole grains, fruits and vegetables contain a variety of fibres and indigestible starches that our body doesn't absorb, but the bacteria in our gut love to eat, and breakfast is a great time to give our gut bacteria a glut of different foods to feed on.

40g (1½oz) amaranth seeds

50g (2oz) roasted almonds

50g (2oz) roasted hazelnuts

50g (2oz) pumpkin seeds

¼ tsp salt

80g (3oz) porridge oats (oatmeal)

100g (3½oz) rolled oats

20g (¾oz) wholemeal plain (whole-wheat all-purpose) flour

1 tsp ground cinnamon

40g (1½oz) vegetable oil

100ml (3½fl oz) honey (I like a dark rich honey)

20 drops of orange oil or the zest of 2 oranges

½ tsp almond extract

1 large egg white, whisked to soft peaks

50g (2oz) dried apricots, finely chopped

50g (2oz) dried sour cherries, finely chopped

50g (2oz) raisins

THIS is granola

Preheat the oven to 150°C fan (170°C/325°F/gas mark 3). Line a large baking tray with baking parchment.

Put a frying pan on a medium–high heat and allow it to heat up. Add a couple of amaranth seeds and see if they start popping after 10–20 seconds. If they do, it is hot enough for you to add the remaining amaranth seeds, cover with a lid and shake the pan. The seeds should start popping within a few seconds. Keep shaking and all the seeds should have popped within 20–30 seconds. Quickly tip into a large mixing bowl (do not leave in the pan as they will burn).

Put the almonds and hazelnuts in the pan and dry-fry until lightly golden (about 5 minutes), keeping an eye on them all the while and shaking the pan occasionally to prevent burning. Transfer these to a food processor immediately. Next toast the pumpkin seeds in the hot pan until they pop. Tip these into the food processor too and pulse a couple of times so the nuts and seeds are broken up but remain chunky.

Put the nuts and seeds into the mixing bowl with the popped amaranth, and add the salt, oats, flour and cinnamon and toss together. In a separate bowl, whisk together the oil, honey, orange oil and almond extract with a fork, then stir this through the mix until it is all coated.

Spread out on the baking tray and bake for 60 minutes (every 15 minutes gently fork through the mix so that it cooks evenly).

Remove the granola from the oven, allow to cool completely, then stir through the apricots, sour cherries and raisins. Store in an airtight container, for up to 1 month.

American pancakes should be light and fluffy, but they should also be quick and easy to rustle up. A sure-fire way to fluffy pancakes is using lots of raising agents, but you can end up with a bitter aftertaste from the baking powder. Whipped egg whites provide a good fluff but they are a faff, however, the addition of sourdough starter is a winner. Sourdough starter is acidic so reacts strongly with the baking powder and gives a good lift. This is also a great way to use up any sourdough starter that you may need to discard when making a loaf. If you don't have a sourdough starter, you can substitute with flour and water, and you may want to add another ½ teaspoon of baking powder to give a boost. Sweet potato adds a gentle sweetness without having to add refined sugar, however these pancakes work just as well as a savoury salty breakfast as they do drizzled with maple syrup and piled with fruit.

70g (2½oz) sweet potato, peeled and chopped into small pieces

100g (3½oz) sourdough starter (or you can substitute with 50g/2oz plain flour and 50g/2oz water)

1 egg

110g (4oz) milk (dairy, oat or soya)

80g (3½oz) plain (all-purpose) flour

20g (¾oz) wholemeal plain (whole-wheat all-purpose) flour

1 tsp baking powder

½ tsp salt

Oil, for greasing

Sourdough sweet tato pancakes

Add the sweet potato to a small saucepan of boiling water, and simmer for 10 minutes until soft and mashable. Drain away the water, then blend the potato with a hand blender until smooth.

In a mixing bowl, whisk together 50g (2oz) of the starter (or flour and water blend), with the egg, milk and blended sweet potato.

In a separate bowl, toss together the plain (all-purpose) flour and the wholemeal (whole-wheat) flour, baking powder and salt.

Add the dry ingredients to the wet mixture and stir until it just comes together (do not overmix). Leave to stand for 15 minutes.

Put a frying pan on a medium heat and lightly grease with oil. Add small ladles of pancake mix to the pan, then once covered in little bubbles, flip over to cook on the other side (about 1 minute each side). Continue until you've finished the mix, then eat straight away with your choice of toppings. I love serving with fruit, Homemade yogurt (see page 43) and honey.

*From left to right:
Breakfast blueberry
muffins (see page 52),
THIS is granola (see
page 44) served with
Home-made yogurt
(see page 43), fresh
berries, watermelon
and peaches.*

I love oats and my workday breakfasts tend to be porridge for the cold months of the year, overnight oats for the warmer months. Both are great because you can pack them with healthy and flavoursome additions. Here I have given you three of my favourite variations that I use a lot (although every time they're slightly different). You can make overnight oats in bulk if you wish. I do two portions at a time and store them in jars in the fridge. The great thing about overnight oats is that you can use lots of different whole grains, not simply oats. Some are best cooked (brown rice, quinoa, buckwheat), but some soften nicely overnight in the mixture (farro, amaranth, millet). If you want to add extra sweeteners, that's up to you, but the oats and milk have a natural sweetness so I don't think this needs it.

Overnight oats

In a bowl, mix together all the base ingredients. It will look very sloppy at this stage, but the oats will soak up a lot of the liquid overnight.

Stir through the extra ingredients that you would like to use, choosing a mix from the fruit, grain/nuts and spice lists. Divide equally among the jars, seal and store in the fridge overnight.

When you're ready to eat, give it a stir and tuck in.

Base	+	Fruit	+	Grains/nuts	+	Spice
40g (1½oz) yogurt (bought or home-made, see page 43)		15g (½oz) dried mango		20g (¾oz) amaranth seeds		½ tsp ground turmeric
+		**or**		**or**		**or**
1 Granny Smith apple, coarsely grated		½ fresh mango (peeled and diced to 1cm/½in pieces)		30g (1oz) cooked brown rice		¼ tsp ground cardamom
+		**or**		**or**		**or**
70g (2½oz) porridge oats (oatmeal)		1 passion fruit		20g (¾oz) chia seeds		¼ tsp ground ginger
+		**or**		10g (¼oz) farro		**or**
70g (2½oz) rolled oats		1 small carrot (finely grated)		**or**		20g (¾oz) nut butter (whichever you like)
+		**or**		2 tsp toasted desiccated (dry unsweetened) coconut		**or**
240ml (9fl oz) milk (whichever milk you prefer)		20g (¾oz) raisins				1 tsp vanilla extract
		or				**or**
		40g (1½oz) frozen raspberries				½ tsp ground cinnamon

I know that porridge is a very simple recipe for a cookbook, but I need to put it in here to show just how simple it is. I have friends and colleagues who still buy exorbitantly over-priced sachets of oat dust sold by big food companies. Please, if you're buying this 'easy' porridge, see how easy it is to make regular porridge. The big bags of cheap porridge oats contain the same (if not better) quality oats than these little packets and it is easy to weigh them out into portions yourself so they're ready to grab and go. For this recipe it is important to make sure you use good-quality chai tea bags to ensure you get lots of flavour.

280ml (9½fl oz) milk
(plant-based or dairy)

1 tsp honey

1 chai tea bag

¼ tsp ground turmeric

5 prunes

45g (1½oz) porridge
oats (oatmeal)

45g (1½oz) frozen blueberries

**Extra additions
(optional):**

1 tsp ground flaxseeds

½ tsp ground ginger

20g (¾oz) cooked brown rice

20g (¾oz) cooked quinoa

Spicy wake-up porridge

Pour the milk into a small saucepan with the honey, chai tea bag and turmeric, and gently heat for 1 minute. Finely chop the prunes (I use scissors), drop them into the milk and simmer for another minute. Add the oats and frozen blueberries to the pan and simmer gently for 3–4 minutes. Let sit for 1 minute and then mix.

If you're using a microwave, put all the ingredients in a bowl and microwave for 30 seconds. Remove, stir, and continue to stir until you have the desired consistency.

Transfer to a bowl and top with whatever you like. I often add a little live natural yogurt and some fresh fruit.

I love a blueberry muffin and a coffee as a weekend breakfast treat. A typical blueberry muffin is simply a cake with very little of anything that will sustain and nourish. These use whizzed-up pears as the main body, which means you're getting one of your portions of fruit and reducing the fat content in the cake in one! They also include lots of different grains that are food for your microbiome, and the blueberries will give you a healthy dose of vitamin C. Top tip: I freeze leftover rice in 25g/1oz portions ready to use for this recipe.

25g (1oz) porridge oats (oatmeal)

1 x 410g (14½oz) can pear halves in fruit juice

75g (3oz) caster (superfine) sugar

25g (1oz) honey

40ml (1½fl oz) light olive oil

25g (1oz) cooked rice

2 eggs

130g (4½oz) plain (all-purpose) flour

50g (2oz) wholemeal plain (whole-wheat all-purpose) flour

15g (½oz) polenta (cornmeal)

10g (¼oz) ground flaxseeds

½ tsp ground cardamom

2 tsp baking powder

150g (5oz) blueberries

Breakfast blueberry muffins

First make a porridge; put the oats in a small saucepan on the lowest heat with 100ml (3½fl oz) of the juice from the can of pears and simmer for 3 minutes until the oats are soft. Add this to a blender with the drained pear halves, sugar, honey, oil and rice, and blend until smooth. Add the eggs and pulse until these are incorporated, too.

Preheat the oven to 180°C fan (200°C/400°F/gas mark 6). Prepare a 12-hole muffin tin with paper cases.

In a mixing bowl, toss together the flours, polenta (cornmeal), ground flaxseeds, cardamom and baking powder. Pour over the blender mixture and stir until combined. Spoon some mixture evenly into each case until a quarter full, drop 3–4 blueberries into each, then top up until three-quarters full.

Bake for 20 minutes or until golden brown on top. They keep well in an airtight container for 2 days, but I advise eating on the first day.

Brunch

*skip breakfast for
mid-morning greatness*

There's always something a bit special about brunch. Perhaps it's because when we brunch (yes, I'm using it as a verb) we can pretend that we're the sort of people who have ample time on our hands. I'm not a particularly stressy person who rushes from one thing to another, but even I notice how time slows down for this meal. Basically, you know you're having a good day when brunch is involved.

Or perhaps it's just because brunch is delicious. Generally more indulgent than the average breakfast, brunch is bigger, heartier and, at the risk of sounding like Nigella, just a little bit racier. The recipe ideas in this chapter hit all those spots, without being too heavy. Where possible, fats and sugars are replaced with other ingredients, without losing that comforting feeling that a good brunch brings. (My Eggs Benedict opposite is the perfect example, using mango to create a smooth sauce instead of the traditional butter hollandaise.)

Brunch tends to be something we go out for – to catch up with friends, maybe – but I really wanted to include a brunch chapter in this book so you don't have to leave the house to get your fix. These recipes are great if you want to invite friends over and impress them with a mid-morning feast. (I'm not a big drinker, but feel free to add a Bloody Mary or two!) Alternatively, you can enjoy a solo brunch, or brunch for the two of you, or prepare enough to have leftovers for tomorrow. These recipe ideas are also great if you exercise on weekend mornings and want a lovely meal prepped for when you get home. For example, with the Tortang talong recipe (kind of like a burnt aubergine omelette, see page 64), you can burn the aubergines before your run or gym session, then make the rest of the dish when you get back.

What about the whole 'skipping breakfast' thing? Well, not everyone wants to eat first thing in the morning, especially if they've got a busy morning routine. Brunch is the ideal solution (whether you make one of these recipes, or simply have your overnight oats or porridge later in the morning, as I often do). There's also some evidence that increasing fasting intervals – which in this case means having your first meal of the day a little later, rather than as soon as you get up – can lead to weight loss and improved health outcomes for some people. It may sound counterintuitive, especially when we've been told all our lives that 'breakfast is the most important meal of the day' (remember, though, that we're often told this by makers of breakfast cereals and snack bars, who are hardly neutral parties). The science is still emerging, but some research suggests that the trillions of microbes that make up the gut microbiome benefit from short periods of fasting. Brunch, then, isn't just a treat for the soul – it could be a treat for your gut, too.

This takes a bit of time and effort, but in my opinion it is worth it. This recipe is made up of a few elements, and you can prepare the sauces in advance, if you like. My muffin recipe overleaf is perfect for these. I am not going to judge you if you buy the muffins, though. The traditional poached eggs are served with a mango sauce that's thick and creamy, but unlike the usual hollandaise it isn't made from butter and egg yolks, so it is far superior because it's low in fat and packed full of vitamins. The chilli sauce is powerful – not in a fiery, hot way, but in its flavour – which complements the muffins, eggs and mango sauce. If you want to really heighten this dish, a generous sprinkling of nutritional dukkah takes it up a notch, adding a tasty crunch.

Mango sauce:

1 ripe mango, peeled and stoned

10ml (¼fl oz) olive oil

1 tsp salt

1 garlic clove

1 tsp white miso paste

10ml (¼fl oz) white wine vinegar

Chilli sauce:

2 garlic cloves

1 chilli (you decide how hot)

2 tbsp olive oil

2 tsp caraway seeds

1 tsp smoked paprika

30ml (1fl oz) lemon juice

2 tbsp tomato paste

1 tbsp maple syrup

To serve:

8 eggs (they need to be fresh, otherwise the white does not hold together)

1 teaspoon vinegar

4 English muffins, store-bought or home-made (see recipe on page 59)

Eggs Benedict with a mango chilli twist

Put all the ingredients for the mango sauce into a blender and pulse until smooth. Set aside at room temperature.

Put all the ingredients for the chilli sauce into a mini food processor and blitz until almost smooth.

For the poached eggs, bring a large saucepan of water to a simmer with the vinegar (you don't want a full boil as this knocks the eggs round too much). Gently crack the eggs into the water and simmer for 4 minutes. Carefully lift out the eggs when cooked to your liking with a slotted spoon and ensure the water drains off.

To eat, cut the muffins in half, toast and spread with the chilli sauce and serve with 2 poached eggs per person, slathered in the mango sauce.

If you have any leftover sauce, this can be kept in the fridge for up to 5 days and be used as a base for salad dressings.

How to make English muffins

140ml (4½fl oz) warm water

30ml (1fl oz) white
wine vinegar

100g (3½oz) yogurt
(bought or home-made,
see page 43)

1 egg

2 tsp instant yeast

300g (10oz) strong white
bread flour, plus extra
for dusting

40g (1½oz) unsalted
butter, softened

1 tsp salt

75g (3oz) strong wholemeal
(whole-wheat) bread flour

60g (2¼oz) amaranth seeds

Put the warm water, vinegar, yogurt, egg, yeast and 100g (3½oz) of the white flour into a bowl, mix, cover and leave in a warm place for 1 hour until bubbly.

Add the softened butter, salt, remaining flours and half of the amaranth seeds to the bowl of a mixer and mix for 10 minutes with a dough hook. This is the easiest method, or you can do it by hand with a spatula. Cover the bowl with beeswax or clingfilm and leave overnight.

In the morning, cut 8 pieces of baking parchment into 15cm (6in) squares. Turn out the dough onto a floured surface and roll out gently to about 1.5cm (¾in) thick. Cut out rounds with an 8cm (4½in) biscuit cutter.

Put the remaining amaranth seeds onto a plate. Place a muffin onto the seeds, then turn over so that some seeds stick to it – you're not looking for a full crust. Repeat with all the remaining muffins.

Place each muffin onto a square of baking parchment and then onto a tray. Leave covered with an oiled piece of cling film in a warm place to rise and double in size, about 45 minutes.

Preheat the oven to 180°C fan (200°C/400°F/gas mark 6).

Heat a heavy-based frying pan on a medium heat. Gently lift a muffin onto a spatula and place in the pan. Add another three, or however many will comfortably fit, and cook, gently turning them over after 3 minutes before cooking the other sides for another 3 minutes.

Transfer to a baking sheet and bake in the oven for a further 10 minutes until golden.

Best used straight away, but any leftover muffins can be sliced in half and stored in the freezer. They can be toasted straight from the freezer.

The history of the bagel is contested, but it is likely to have developed from the Polish obwarzanek krakowski or the German pretzel hundreds of years ago. They are poached after proving and before baking in the oven. This gives the bagel that distinct chew, and if poached in a bath of lye it will develop a brown lacquered crust. Lye is a toxic and corrosive alkaline chemical that isn't easily available to home cooks; bicarbonate of soda is a weaker alkali, but a lot safer to use at home, and use sticky malt extract to give a sweet brown crust you can be proud of.

This recipe uses a 10-hour overnight prove in the fridge, which is perfect for ensuring you get fresh bagels baked ready for breakfast. A word of warning, you need to stretch the hole in the middle of the bagel a lot wider than you think as it will close up on proving and baking.

Morning baked bagels

1 tbsp malt extract

50g (2oz) prunes

225g (8oz) warm water

350g (12oz) strong white bread flour

50g (2oz) strong wholemeal (whole-wheat) bread flour

4g instant yeast

6g fine salt

20g (¾oz) poppy seeds

1 tsp vegetable oil

For the poaching pot:

2 tbsp malt extract

½ tsp bicarbonate of soda (baking soda)

To finish:

Caraway seeds

Sesame seeds

In a mixing bowl, using a hand blender or food processor, blend together the malt extract, prunes and warm water until combined and smooth.

Put the flours, yeast, salt and poppy seeds into a large mixing bowl, add the wet mixture and mix to form a dough. Knead for 5 minutes in the bowl, then leave, covered with beeswax cloth, clingfilm or a tea towel, for 30 minutes.

Divide the dough into 6 pieces (each about 110g/4oz). Shape each piece into a tight ball. Shape your bagel by sticking your finger through the middle and stretch it outwards (you want it to be twice as wide as you would like the final hole, as it will rise when baked).

Place the bagels on a baking parchment-lined tray, pour the oil onto a piece of cling film and wipe it across the whole surface. Now cover the bagels with this and place in the fridge for about 10 hours.

The next morning, preheat the oven to 180°C fan (200°C/400°F/gas mark 6).

Fill a large saucepan with 2 litres (3½ pints) of water and the malt extract and bring to the boil. Reduce to a simmer and add the bicarbonate of soda (make sure you've turned the heat down as the bicarb will make the water foam and overflow if it is still boiling). Drop in each bagel and poach for 45 seconds on each side. Place the poached bagels on a baking parchment-lined tray, sprinkle with the caraway and sesame seeds, and bake for 18 minutes.

Place the bagels on a wire rack to cool. Store in an airtight container for up to 2 days, or slice in half and freeze. They can be toasted from frozen.

These pancakes are not just a feast for you, but a picnic for your microbiome, too. The batter features lots of different grains that provide indigestible starches. Indigestible starches are the starches in whole grains that are not absorbed into the body by our small intestine. They pass through to our large intestine, but they are not wasted, because good bacteria love to feed on them and produce all kinds of compounds that our body uses. The filling is packed with good bacteria and bacteria-friendly foods, but most of all it is packed with flavour. I have a group of friends who enjoy going out for a weekend morning run, followed by brunch. This recipe is great as you can rustle up the batter before the run, and it's ready for you when you return.

serves 4

100g (3½oz) buckwheat flour

20g (¾oz) wholemeal plain (whole-wheat all-purpose) flour

25g (1oz) millet

5g (1/8 oz) ground flaxseeds

100g (3½oz) sourdough starter (see page 23, or 50g/2oz of plain flour, and 50ml/2fl oz water)

½ tsp instant yeast (if you're not using sourdough starter, add another ½ tsp yeast)

1 egg

300ml (10fl oz) warm water

Olive oil, for frying

Filling:

70g (2½oz) unpasteurised blue cheese

30g (1oz) live natural yogurt (see page 43 for home-made)

¼ tsp wasabi powder/paste

½ tsp flaky sea salt

10g (¼oz) fresh dill leaves

150g (5oz) mushrooms

10ml (¼fl oz) olive oil

1 garlic clove, minced

4 eggs

100g (3½oz) cooked beetroot (in vinegar, if preferred), cut into small cubes

3 spring onions (scallions), sliced

Biome buckwheat pancakes

Mix all the pancake ingredients together in a bowl and leave, covered, on the countertop, for 1 hour.

When the batter is almost ready, blend the cheese, yogurt and wasabi together, then mix in the salt and dill leaves. Gently fry the mushrooms in a glug of olive oil until browned (5 minutes), then stir through the garlic and set aside. Finally fry the 4 eggs (however you like them), transfer to a plate and set aside.

Put a non-stick frying pan on a medium–high heat, lightly grease with olive oil, then pour in a ladle of batter.

Cook for 2–3 minutes without being tempted to poke around at the pancake, then gently flip.

Once on the other side, cover half the pancake with a quarter of the fillings – scatter the mushrooms, beetroot and spring onions, add one egg and spread the other half with the whipped cheese mixture. Gently fold in half and slide onto a plate. Repeat for the other 3 pancakes.

Tortang talong translates as aubergine cake, but they are more like an omelette, and they are a favourite of mine. In the Philippines these are eaten at any time of the day, often pimped up with ground meat, mushrooms or green beans if they're prepared for dinner or a main dish. I like to prepare the aubergines in advance and rustle up this dish with a bowl of steaming jasmine rice.

A burnt smoky aubergine is a dream for me — I love almost anything smoked. To smoke the flesh of an aubergine you don't need any fancy equipment, as it comes with a strong skin that, once heated, acts as its own smoker. Simply put an aubergine directly onto a flame, and once black and burnt the flesh inside should be soft and smoky.

This is a great healthy brunch that does not scrimp on flavour and substance. Aubergines are a good source of B vitamins, potassium and fibre, and this recipe includes quinoa, which boosts the protein content.

serves 2

4 Asian aubergines (small and thin), or 2 regular aubergines (eggplants)

50g (2oz) sesame seeds

Toasted sesame oil, for frying

4 eggs

1 tsp salt

100g (3½oz) cooked quinoa

Dipping sauce:

3 tbsp light soy sauce

Juice of ½ lime

1 tbsp honey

1 garlic clove, minced

½ red chilli, deseeded and finely sliced

Tortang talong

Burn the aubergines either under a grill or over an open flame, holding them with metal tongs and turning them until the skins are black all over and steam is coming out of the middle (about 6–8 minutes). Allow to cool slightly, peel off the skin (leaving the stalk in place) and set aside. If you are using regular aubergines, cut them in half, making sure you retain half the stalk for each side.

In a dry frying pan, toast the sesame seeds on a medium heat until they are golden. Remove from the pan straight away (otherwise they will keep on colouring), transfer to a bowl and set aside.

Put the dipping sauce ingredients into a small jar and shake to combine.

Heat a non-stick frying pan and grease with the sesame oil. In a bowl, whisk the first egg with ¼ teaspoon of salt and 25g (1oz) of the cooked quinoa. Place the first burnt aubergine into the pan and press down with a fork to fan out the flesh. Pour over the egg mixture, sprinkle with sesame seeds, and fry until golden brown underneath (about 2 minutes). Flip and cook for a further minute on the other side.

Repeat with the other aubergines and eggs, then serve immediately with the dipping sauce.

Morning baked bagels (see page 60) served with cream cheese, smoked salmon, avocado and lemon.

Dark chocolate

Years ago, I lived in Côte d'Ivoire, where one-third of the world's cacao is harvested. I saw a lot of cocoa beans while I was there. Cocoa beans, or cacao beans, are the dried, fermented seeds found inside cacao pods (which, weirdly, grow off the cacao tree's trunk, not its branches). I remember helping a friend with the drying process. The beans were spread out on the red clay earth and dried in the sun. We shuffled our feet through the beans, keeping our soles on the ground, to tumble and mix the beans so they dried out evenly.

From food of the gods to meat – chocolate hybrid horrors: the evolution of chocolate

Chocolate can be traced back as far as the Mayans and Aztecs, who consumed it in drink form and believed it was a gift from the gods. (Theobroma, the botanical name for the cacao tree, means 'food of the gods'. Is it any wonder we worship chocolate?) But it was the English who invented chocolate bars.

In 1847 the Fry family discovered that if you take cocoa, add some extra cocoa butter and a little sugar, you get a solid bar of chocolate. Cadbury and Rowntree's followed suit, and these three English Quaker families were responsible for the birth of chocolate bars as we know them today. Milk chocolate was made possible by the invention of powdered milk, and it was someone at Nestlé who first suggested mixing their milk powder into chocolate.

As a keen cyclist, I was interested to learn from chocolate historian Alex Hutchinson that in the 1890s Rowntree's created a product called Oxcholate – a blend of meat and chocolate aimed at 'travellers, invalids and cyclists'. Although I prefer mine without the meat, a little pre-cycling dark chocolate isn't as odd as it sounds; the theobromine compound found in chocolate has a similar effect on the body as caffeine, and can be considered a stimulant! Dark chocolate is also high in polyphenols, which promote the growth of healthy gut bacteria. So whether you're a cyclist or not, a little dark chocolate is definitely good for you.

How to use this hero ingredient

What percentage of cocoa solids makes a chocolate dark? I'd say 70% as a minimum. (For me, the bitterer the better. Even as a child I preferred dark chocolate to milk.)

Chocolate contains emulsifiers, so when you add melted dark chocolate to other recipes it can help to emulsify the mix, as in my Dark choc energy balls. Cocoa powder adds a rich depth of flavour to bakes, but sometimes the chocolatey taste gets lost. If you're after a strong chocolatey hit, try working in some dark chocolate chunks. Cacao nibs are pieces of the original cacao seed after roasting, which have a slightly barky texture, but after you've crunched into one you get a blast of intense dark chocolate flavour, which I love.

You'll find dark chocolate in my:

- Banana chocolate muffins (see page 214)
- Dark choc energy balls (see page 208)
- Notella swirls (see page 72)

The 'fika' tradition in Sweden is a popular ritual where you gather for a coffee break to catch up with friends or family and enjoy – usually – a cinnamon bun. Cinnamon rolls are a speciality of mine . . . at one job I was officially allowed to arrive late for work if I brought a tray of cinnamon rolls for the team. The classic American way to make them is with an enriched dough, but this dough is naturally sweetened with grated carrot. I realised that with carrot and cinnamon I only needed raisins, walnuts and a vanilla icing to get the traditional carrot cake flavours that I love.

550g (1lb 4oz) strong white bread flour, plus extra for dusting

7g instant yeast

4g salt

80g (3oz) peeled carrot, grated

10 drops of orange oil (or the zest of 1 orange)

70g (2½oz) unsalted butter (at room temperature)

70g (2½oz) light soft brown sugar

4 tsp ground cinnamon

40g (1½oz) raisins

40g (1½oz) chopped walnuts

Glaze:

3 tsp soft brown sugar

1 tsp malt extract

50ml (2fl oz) water

Icing:

50g (2oz) unsalted butter, softened

50g (2oz) icing (confectioners') sugar

1 tsp vanilla extract

Carrot cakey cinnamon rolls

Put the flour, yeast and salt into a large mixing bowl. Into a jug add 300ml (10fl oz) of warm water (about 30°C/86°F) and the grated carrot. Pour the wet mixture into the dry and bring together to form a sticky dough. Cover with beeswax cloth or clingfilm and leave for 10 minutes.

Gently knead the dough in the bowl for 30 seconds, then cover and leave in a warm place until the dough has doubled in size (about 1 hour). Prepare a traybake tin with baking parchment (I scrunch it into a ball then press it into the tin to make sure it goes into all the corners).

Tip the dough onto a lightly floured surface and fold the dough in on itself a couple of times, rotating 90 degrees each time to form a crude square. Roll the dough out to about 50cm x 40cm (20in x 16in). Do not push too hard. Dough is elastic and so sometimes it is best to roll a couple of times, then let the dough relax for a minute before rolling again.

Beat the orange oil into the butter and spread over the dough, then sprinkle with the sugar. Dust with the cinnamon and sprinkle over the raisins. Start at one of the shorter sides and tightly roll the dough into a long sausage. Using a very sharp knife, cut into 12 pieces and arrange in the tray. Make sure the cut side is facing up. Cover with cling film and leave to rise until doubled in size in a warm place (about 45 minutes).

Preheat the oven to 200°C fan (220°C/425°F/gas mark 7) and bake for 15–20 minutes.

In a small saucepan, mix the glaze ingredients. Bring to a simmer, and when the bubbles get bigger you'll have a syrup. Brush onto the buns while still warm. Sprinkle with the walnut pieces.

When the buns are cool, in a bowl, beat the icing ingredients and ice the buns however you want, then eat the same day.

Ever since I started making cinnamon rolls I've been obsessed with bread enclosing a spiral of filling. I first made this recipe when a friend told me she loved the look of my cinnamon rolls but hated raisins and cinnamon, and she was vegan. I'd just made some chocolate and hazelnut spread and realised that creamy, chocolatey goodness would work perfectly in a swirl of soft bread. The Japanese yundane method is used here to get a soft dough; boiling water is added to bread flour to gelatinise the starches, allowing them to absorb more water and increase the water content of the dough.

You won't believe how easy it is to make your own chocolate and hazelnut spread until you've given it a go. It tastes even better than the well-known shop-bought version, which is essentially oil and glucose syrup. Using silken tofu rather than butter to make icing is a nutritious – and vegan-friendly – option, plus it's virtually fat-free. The main problem with these swirls is that you won't be able to eat only one of them.

Dough:

450g (1lb) strong white bread flour, plus extra for dusting

50g (2oz) strong wholemeal (whole grain) bread flour

7g instant yeast

8g salt

350g (12oz) water

Chocolate and hazelnut spread:

75g (3oz) toasted hazelnuts

¼ tsp salt

100g (3½oz) chocolate (I use 70% cocoa solids, check it is vegan)

1 tsp vanilla bean paste

20ml (¾fl oz) maple syrup

50ml (2fl oz) oat milk

Icing:

100g (3½oz) silken tofu (bean curd)

1 tsp lemon juice

1 tsp vanilla bean paste

100g (3½oz) icing (confectioners') sugar

25g (1oz) coconut oil, softened

Notella swirls

Line a traybake tin with baking parchment.

To make the yundane mix, weigh out 100g (3½oz) of the white flour and pour over 120g (4oz) boiling water. Mix to a paste or dough, cover and set aside for 1 hour.

While you are waiting you can make the chocolate and hazelnut spread. Toast the hazelnuts in a dry frying pan until golden (keep an eye on them as they burn easily). Tip them straight into a food processor and blitz until they reach a fine powder or come together to a butter (this may take 3–5 minutes).

Melt the chocolate in a bain-marie and pour this over the nuts. Continue to blitz in the processor until smooth then add the vanilla, maple syrup and oat milk and blitz again until really smooth.

In a large mixing bowl, add the rest of the flour, the yeast, salt, 180g (6oz) of warm water and then the yundane mix. Mix together in the bowl until it forms a sticky dough, then leave covered for 10 minutes.

Knead the dough in the bowl for 3–5 minutes (do not add any flour), then leave, covered, in a warm spot until doubled in size (about 1 hour).

After proving the dough, tip it out onto a lightly floured surface and roll it out to 50cm x 50cm (20in x 20in). Take your time with this, dough is very elastic but if you continue it will stretch to the square shape you want.

Spread all over with the chocolate and hazelnut spread and roll from the top down until you have a long sausage. Divide the dough into 12 pieces and slice through the roll. Do not press down with the knife otherwise you'll destroy the swirl. You need a sharp knife or a good bread knife. Place the dough end down into the tin, cover with oiled cling film, and put in a warm place to rise until doubled in size (about 45 minutes).

Preheat the oven to 180°C fan (200°C/400°F/gas mark 6). Bake the rolls for 15 minutes until golden on top.

While the rolls are baking, whisk the tofu, lemon juice, vanilla and icing (confectioners') sugar until smooth, then add the softened coconut oil and whisk again until combined. Transfer to a piping bag and chill until the mixture has thickened (about 30 minutes).

Remove the rolls from the oven and leave to cool on a wire rack. Once cool, pipe the tofu icing on top as you wish and eat while they're lovely and fresh.

I've worked hard to try to get a really good chocolate bread that isn't too sweet or rich. To get bakes really chocolatey you often need lots of cream, butter, sugar or eggs to bring the cocoa powder to life. This works well for a Sachertorte or a chocolate mud cake, but I like to do things a little more healthily. The answer is dark chocolate chunks to give the well-known chocolate hit, then a rich and earthy crumb with malt extract, cocoa and coffee. Sweetness comes from the raisins and the buns are finished with a panettone-style crust made with egg whites and ground almonds. These buns are a great way of using up any sourdough starter discard you may have.

100g (3½oz) sourdough starter (see page 23, or 50g/2oz strong white bread flour, and add 50g/2oz to the warm water)

200g (7oz) warm water

3g instant yeast

2 tsp malt extract

1 tsp instant coffee granules

1 egg yolk

300g (10oz) strong white bread flour

60g (2oz) strong wholemeal (whole-wheat) bread flour

30g (1oz) cocoa powder

1 tsp salt

100g (3½oz) raisins

100g (3½oz) dark chocolate (70% cocoa solids), cut into rough chunks

Topping:

30g (1oz) caster (superfine) sugar

1 egg white

5g cocoa powder

30g (1oz) ground almonds

10g (¼oz) cornflour (cornstarch)

20g (¾oz) flaked (slivered) almonds

20g (¾oz) cacao nibs

Real chocolate buns

Combine the sourdough starter (or use flour and water, see left), warm water, yeast, malt extract, coffee granules, egg yolk and 100g (3½oz) of the white bread flour in a mixing bowl. Mix to a porridge consistency, cover with a clean tea towel and leave for 1 hour in a warm place.

Add the remaining flours, cocoa powder and salt and bring together to form a dough in the bowl. Leave for 10 minutes then knead in the bowl for 1 minute. Cover and leave in a warm place until doubled in size (about 1 hour).

Knock back the dough in the bowl and gently knead in the raisins and chocolate pieces to evenly distribute them through the dough.

Divide the dough into 8 100g (3½oz) pieces and roll each into a tight ball. Place on a lined baking tray 2cm (¾in) apart. Cover with oiled cling film and leave to rise until doubled in size (about 1 hour, but this might take longer than a regular bread dough).

Preheat the oven to 200°C fan (220°C/425°F/gas mark 7).

While the oven heats, make the topping. In a bowl, mix the sugar, egg white, cocoa powder, ground almonds and cornflour (cornstarch) together, then brush or spoon this mix onto the top of each roll. Decorate with the almonds and cacao nibs, then bake for 12–15 minutes until they have a nice crust and sound hollow when tapped.

Allow to cool on the tray for 1 minute, then transfer to a wire rack to cool completely. They are best eaten fresh, but they can be stored in an airtight container for up to 2 days, or frozen. They are nice toasted, too.

Dips and dippers

dip in and out
all day long

If you're a snacker, welcome home. This chapter is for you.

Quick, portable and moreish, dips and dippers are my go-to snack. But while shop-bought dips are often full of salt, preservatives and ingredients that I can't even pronounce let alone want to put in my mouth, the dips in this chapter are full of nutritious ingredients. In other words, I can feel good about slathering them on as thickly as I like. I've also found that crackers are an easy way to get more whole grains and seeds into my diet (either by adding them into the mixture or sprinkling them on top). Add the two together and you have a satisfying, healthy way to fill the hungry gap. Something you can have on hand when you're working from home, or to take into the office for a mid-afternoon desk picnic.

Dips and crackers also make a great start to a meal with friends – something laidback but tasty to have on the table when people arrive. There's not much effort involved but your guests will feel like you're really treating them. It's a bit like baking bread for someone – simple, but it shows you care.

And it's so hard to get bored of dips, thanks to the huge variety available. You could, if you were so inclined, draw a map of the world that's marked not by geographical borders, but by dip preferences. So wherever you travel, especially if you're lucky enough to share a communal meal with locals, there will probably be some sort of dip-and-dipper combination on the table.

A word on how to use the dips and crackers in this chapter. You can, of course, just spread any of the dips onto any of the crackers (or dunk any of the crackers into any of the dips, if that's how you roll). But I also love the crackers paired with a nut butter and a square of dark chocolate if I have some leftover and can't be bothered to make a fresh dip. What's more, I think the dips work well not just as a snack, but as an everyday condiment. They're great for dolloping onto meals or salads to add a different texture or temperature, or even just to bring a boring dish to life. My cooling cucumber dip on top of a curry? Heaven. Classic salsa (see page 87) or Pickley guacamole (see page 92) on a veggie burger? Sure, why not? Spicy roasted houmous (see page 91) on top of, well, everything? Absolutely. With a few good dip recipes under your belt, you have a whole new repertoire of ways to liven up your everyday meals.

I never want to eat the last section of a loaf when a new one is coming out of the oven. My first thought is to turn it into breadcrumbs, but there are only so many bags of breadcrumbs that can fit into my freezer, and this is a dilemma I come up against most weeks. My next thought is to turn them into crackers. You have to be pretty dextrous to cut 3mm slices from a loaf to make crackers, but with stale bread and a really good bread knife it is do-able.

About 10 slices of old bread (depends on the size of the bread)

15ml (½fl oz) olive oil

1 egg white

Mixed seeds of your choice

Flaky sea salt

Last of the loaf crackers

As you find that your bread is not as fresh as you would like, slice it into 3mm slices, then pop them into a freezer bag, separating them with sheets of baking parchment, and store in the freezer. Once you have collected about 10 slices, remove and allow to defrost at room temperature.

Preheat the oven to 180°C fan (200°C/400°F/gas mark 6).

Once defrosted, slice into cracker shapes and brush one side with olive oil and the other side with egg white. Place the cracker olive-oil-side down onto a lined baking tray, sprinkle with seeds and salt on the upper egg-white side, then bake in the oven for 10 minutes until golden brown.

Allow to cool on a wire rack. They are best if eaten within 2 days, but can last a week. If storing, always allow to cool completely and keep in an airtight container.

Firstly, can I just say, crackers are not boring. I feel that the cracker is sometimes relegated to simply a vehicle to carry cheese, but they are so much more than that. I love eating them with peanut butter (although I fear I may be alone in this one, I am frequently told that a dry cracker mixed with peanut butter makes a peanuty cement). Broken-up crackers are great for providing texture on top of salads, but also crumbled onto pasta, dahl or soups. Then there are dips…! So really, crackers are versatile and if you're a sourdough baker, a great way to use your discard.

Sourdough starter is already an elastic mixture, so with the addition of a couple of ingredients the dough can be rolled really thin to provide the perfect snap. I like to pass these through my pasta machine to get paper-thin crackers, but if you're rolling by hand, thicker crackers still work well. You can source charcoal powder from specialist food stores, or easily online, but it is not an essential ingredient, it's simply here to give an interesting colour. You can leave this out and still get a great cracker.

100g (3½oz) sourdough starter (see page 23, or 50g/2oz strong white bread flour and 50ml/2fl oz water)

20g (¾oz) strong white bread flour, plus extra for dusting

40g (1½oz) wholemeal (whole-wheat) flour

5g activated charcoal powder

10g (¼oz) olive oil

3g salt

Sesame seeds and flaky sea salt, for topping

Crispy charcoal crackers

In a small bowl, mix all the cracker ingredients together (except the toppings) until it forms a dough. Knead for 1 minute in the bowl, then wrap in cling film and chill in the fridge for 1 hour.

Divide the dough into 3 pieces, then on a lightly floured surface roll out each piece into a long oblong 2mm thick. I use my pasta machine for this; if you don't have a pasta machine it will take a lot of rolling.

Preheat the oven to 180°C fan (200°C/400°F/gas mark 6). Line a baking tray with baking parchment.

Sprinkle the top of the dough with the seeds, then press them into the dough gently with a rolling pin. Next, spray or brush the crackers lightly with water, leave for 10 seconds, then sprinkle on the flaky salt. Cut up however you like. I love straight geometric lines contrasting with the rough outer edges. Transfer to the baking tray and bake for 10 minutes.

Once out of the oven, allow to cool on the tray and crisp up. They are best if eaten within 2 days, but they can last a week. If storing, always allow to cool completely then keep in an airtight container.

Good grissini are crisp, crunchy and salty, and maybe a little soft and chewy on the inside. I love whipping up a batch of these and eating them while they are still warm with a chilled Gazpacho or the simpler cold tomato soup, Salmorejo (see page 108). The addition of amaranth seeds with the polenta (cornmeal) makes them really crunchy, and gives a nutritious seedy boost. You can sub in your favourite olives and you can also add small cubes of cheese, if you wish. The rye flour makes the dough very sticky, but don't worry, it is not a dough you handle too much.

250g (9oz) plain (all-purpose) flour, plus extra for dusting

50g (2oz) rye flour

1 tsp salt

7g instant yeast

80ml (3½oz) olive oil

170ml (6fl oz) lukewarm semi-skimmed (skimmed) milk

150g (5oz) Kalamata olives, stoned and finely chopped (or your choice of olives, any will work)

50g (2oz) coarse polenta (cornmeal)

30g (1oz) amaranth seeds

Flaky sea salt, for topping

Rye Kalamata grissini

Mix the flours, salt and yeast in a bowl. Add the olive oil, milk and olives and bring together to a sticky dough. Cover and allow to rest for 5 minutes. Knead gently for 3 minutes in the bowl. It is very sticky so this usually means just pushing it around. Try to get as much off your hands as possible, then cover with a beeswax cloth or clingfilm and leave to prove for 1 hour in a warm place.

Preheat the oven to 170°C fan (190°C/375°F/gas mark 5).

Roll out the dough as a rectangle on a floured surface (30cm x 50cm/ 12in x 20in and about 1cm/½in thick). Cut into 1cm (½in) strips, then leave to sit for 5 minutes. Spritz with a water spray and allow to stand for 30 seconds until they become tacky. Sprinkle the polenta (cornmeal) and amaranth on a tray and gently roll each strip in them to form breadsticks. Finally, sprinkle over some flaky sea salt.

Place on a lined tray and bake for 25 minutes, or until they become your preferred shade of golden. These are best eaten fresh but stored in an airtight container, these will keep for up to 3 days.

A crunchy crudité with a creamy dip is great as a summer appetiser. These poached vegetables retain a lovely crunch and their natural flavours are heightened with a gentle pickling. There is a general assumption that raw vegetables are better for you. It is true that boiling can reduce vitamin content, but it is not always so simple. The provitamin beta carotene, for example, is more readily available in cooked carrots because vegetables often have a matrix wall that needs to be disrupted for our bodies to get a good dose.

I always make a double portion of these poached veg, then use them as a salad topper, too. Also, please don't discard the pickling liquor, as you can use this for the Pickled cabbage parcels (see page 157), or to make more pickled poached vegetables. You can store the pickling liquor in the fridge for up to a month.

Poaching liquor:

500ml (16fl oz) water

100ml (3½fl oz) white
wine vinegar

100ml (3½fl oz) lemon juice

3 bay leaves

2 celery sticks

1 cheek of a green (bell)
pepper

20g (¾oz) fresh parsley

1 tsp salt

Vegetables:

100g (3½oz) baby carrots,
cut in half (or batons if using
large carrots)

100g (3½oz) Romanesco,
cut into florets

75g (3oz) fennel, cut into
2cm (¾in) chunks

75g (3oz) asparagus, trimmed

50g (2oz) spring onions, cut
into 4cm (1½in) lengths

Pickled poached vegetables

Put all the poaching liquor ingredients in a medium saucepan, bring to a simmer and cook for 10 minutes.

Add the carrots and Romanesco to the liquor in the pan and simmer for 3 minutes. Add the rest of the vegetables and simmer for another 3 minutes. Remove from the liquor with a slotted spoon (you can save the liquor in a jar to use again). Refresh the vegetables in a bowl of cold water and drain. Serve immediately with your favourite dip.

Loads of garlic cloves whizzed together with anchovies and glugs of olive oil – sounds strange, but a creamy bagna càuda is something to behold. I love eating this with crackers, poached vegetables and crudités. This recipe will make a good sharing portion, so it's perfect as an appetiser for guests. I often make a half portion for myself to munch on as a snack, then use the remaining bagna càuda as a dressing for my salad. This is a rich dip and high in fat, but the fats are oh so good for you – anchovies are rich in omega-3 fatty acids and olive oil is full of phenolic antioxidants.

100g (3½oz) garlic cloves (middle stems removed if they're thick or green)

250ml (9fl oz) semi-skimmed milk

20g (¾fl oz) fresh breadcrumbs

50g (2oz) anchovies, drained

40ml (1½fl oz) olive oil

10ml (¼fl oz) lemon juice

Salt (optional)

Bagna càuda

Put the garlic in a small saucepan with 200ml (7fl oz) water. Bring to a simmer then drain off and discard the water. Refill the pan, do this again, discarding the water a second time.

Now add the milk to the pan with the garlic and bring to a simmer, then cook the garlic for 8 minutes until soft (be careful not to scorch the milk). Tip this into a blender with the breadcrumbs and anchovies and blend until smooth. Slowly add the oil and lemon juice while blending.

Scoop into a bowl and serve warm or cover and chill it until required. Store in the fridge for up to a week.

Salsa is a great way to boost your vegetable intake and give a fresh bite to a heavy meal. It's a question of personal preference; tomatoes form the base, but all further additions are a point of taste. I'm not going to tell you to add sweetcorn or pineapple, as this is up to you, but there are some top tips that can help any fresh salsa. Firstly, deseeding the tomatoes — you don't want a watery salsa and the seeds are covered in gelatinous membranes that can make your salsa sloppy. Do not discard the seeds, though, you can throw these into a soup, tomato sauce or stock. Secondly, soaking your onions in cold water will preserve that crispy bite. And finally, do not add the salt until a few minutes before eating, or it will draw out all the water in the tomatoes and you will be serving a watery salsa. My final top tip would be to use really good tomatoes, for the best flavour.

½ medium onion,
   finely chopped

4 large plum tomatoes,
   deseeded and cut into
   ½cm (¼in) chunks

1 pickled chilli, or a
   fresh jalapeño chilli,
   finely chopped

1 garlic clove, minced

15ml (½fl oz) fresh lime juice

½ tsp salt

½ tsp white miso

10g (¼oz) fresh coriander
   (cilantro), stalks and leaves,
   finely chopped

Classic salsa

Add the onion to a bowl and cover with cold water.

Put the tomatoes into another bowl with the finely chopped chilli and mix through the garlic.

Mix the lime juice, salt and miso in a bowl and set aside.

When you're ready to eat, drain the onion and add to the tomatoes. Stir through the lime juice mix and finally stir through the coriander (cilantro). Serve immediately.

Clockwise from left to right: Crispy charcoal crackers (see page 80) and Pickled poached vegetables (see page 84), Silken cucumber dip (see page 90), Rye Kalamata grissini (see page 82), Spicy roasted houmous (see page 91), Pickley guacamole (see page 92).

Cool and refreshing, this dip can stand alone slathered on crackers or crudités, or be used to calm down a fiery curry or smooth off a spicy wrap. Versatility in dips is essential for me, as the last thing you want is to have a jar of dip sitting at the back of the fridge. It takes a bit of effort to squeeze the water from the cucumber in this recipe, but it is worth it as this ensures the dip remains creamy and crunchy. I've kept this herb-free, but swapping the cumin seeds for a big handful of dill will make it taste fresh and great to spread on sandwiches. Most creamy dips are made with high-fat mayo, cream or cream cheese, or if you go for a low-fat version it'll be full of thickeners, emulsifiers and starches. Using tofu means you get a low-fat dip that is vegan, creamy and gives a good portion of protein.

2 tsp cumin seeds

200g (7oz) silken tofu

20ml (¾fl oz) olive oil

20ml (¾fl oz) lemon juice

1 tsp salt

1 garlic clove, minced

1 cucumber (about 350g/12oz), peeled and seeds removed

Silken cucumber dip

Toast the cumin seeds in a dry frying pan for about a minute, tossing them occasionally, until they start to smell citrusy. Immediately transfer to a bowl and set aside.

Whizz the tofu, olive oil, lemon juice, salt and garlic in a bowl with a hand-held blender until smooth.

Coarsely grate the cucumber flesh into a sieve and squeeze hard between your hands to remove excess water. Tip into a bowl and mix with all the other ingredients, then transfer to a jar, seal, and keep in the fridge ideally for 24 hours, but you can eat this after an hour, too. This will keep in the fridge for up to 5 days.

(See image on pages 88–89.)

When I was a kid houmous was not a staple, but now there are very few things I do not slather in its creamy, salty goodness. There are many recipes claiming to be the perfect one, and I do agree that the best houmous is made from soaking and then simmering dried chickpeas, but this quick version is also delicious. Once you've made your own you'll see how easy it is, and how superior it is to shop-bought versions. Gochujang is a fermented chilli paste from Korea and is a staple in my fridge. It has rich, sweet, spicy and earthy notes that both punch and hug your taste buds. You can use other chilli sauces/pastes, but once you've tried gochujang you'll be ditching the rest and using it to enliven lots of your favourite meals.

Topping:

40ml (1½fl oz) olive oil

½ tsp salt

2 tsp gochujang paste

½ aubergine (eggplant), cut into 1cm (½in) chunks

1 red (bell) pepper, cut into 1cm (½in) chunks

½ x 400g (15oz) can chickpeas, drained (keep the liquid for other recipes, page 205)

5 garlic cloves

Houmous:

1½ x 400g (15oz) cans chickpeas (about 350g/12oz drained weight), drained (keep the liquid for other recipes, see page 205)

10ml (¼fl oz) lemon juice

½ tsp salt

50g (2oz) light tahini

1 garlic clove

Spicy roasted houmous

Preheat the oven to 180°C fan (200°C/400°F/gas mark 6).

Mix the oil with the salt and gochujang paste and spread over the bottom of a large baking tray.

Toss the aubergine (eggplant) and pepper through the oil. Sprinkle over the chickpeas and the garlic cloves (still in their skins). Roast for 30 minutes, or until the edges of the peppers char (I fork through the mix twice during the cooking time as the pieces at the edges tend to brown quicker). Once out of the oven, allow to cool.

Put all the houmous ingredients into a food processor. Take the roasted garlic cloves from the tray and squeeze the insides out into the food processor. Next, pour all the excess oil from the baking tray into the mix and blend. You'll need to add a little cold water to ensure you get the right consistency. How much water you add is down to your personal preference, but once the houmous sits it will thicken up (I usually add about 100ml/3½fl oz). Transfer to a container and top with the roasted veg. Store in the fridge in an airtight container and use within a week.

(See image on pages 88–89.)

There are a few important factors that I consider when making a really good guacamole. Firstly, you need a ripe avocado. Secondly, you need to take the time to remove the seeds from the tomatoes otherwise the dip becomes too watery, and finally you need to get the perfect balance of garlic and salt. The pickled chillies lift the guacamole and give it an extra dimension. If you don't have pickled chillies, you can use a single fresh chilli, or use pickled onions too. They provide a zing, which means the usual lime juice is not required. When I lived in Malawi we had our own avocado tree that dripped with sun-ripened, almost buttery fruit. I pine for the days when I could make a bowl of this daily.

1 ripe avocado, peeled and stoned

20ml (¾fl oz) olive oil

½ tsp salt

1 small garlic clove, minced

2 medium tomatoes

About 10 pickled chillies (depending on how hot your chillies are, and how hot you can handle)

Pickley guacamole

Put half the avocado into a jug and smash the other half with a fork on a plate. Add the oil, salt and garlic to the avocado in the jug, then blend with a hand blender until smooth. Mix the blended and mashed avocado together.

Finely chop the tomatoes (remove the seeds and keep these to add to a sauce another time). Finely chop the pickled chillies, then add these to the avocado with the tomatoes. Serve straight away. This will keep in the fridge for up to 3 days.

Soup to go

*make it when you
have time, eat it
when you don't*

Let's be honest, soup has a bit of a dowdy reputation. (As demonstrated by the film *Juno*, where Michael Cera says he doesn't like a girl at school because 'she smells like soup'.) Soup is the unfun person at the party. It's the thing you turn to when you can't think of anything else to eat, when you're ill on the sofa, or when life has kicked you in the teeth.

Except, I love soup. I could eat soup for lunch, for dinner, when I'm poorly, when I'm happy, even when I'm on holiday. I could eat it as a simple meal, or (if you'll excuse the pun) souped-up into an impressive dinner. In fact, some of my best dinner parties have involved a steaming pan of soup for everyone to ladle into their bowls, and a table covered with breads, spreads, dips, crackers and cheeses.

One thing I love about soup is it's so versatile. A soup can be light and silky or chunky and substantial. There are hot soups for those autumn and winter months, or chilled soups that are perfect for summer, when (if you're like me) you're often more thirsty than hungry. (On that subject, I'm really bad at staying hydrated, and I've found soup – in any form – is an easy way to boost my hydration at lunchtime.) Soup is also great for packing loads of veggies, grains or pulses into every serving, giving you a shot of vitamins and fibre. And it's so easy to make.

You can rustle up a good soup quickly, but many soups benefit from a little time to let the flavours develop. (Or in the case of cold soups like Gazpacho and Salmorejo, see page 108, time to chill properly. A cold soup that isn't fully cold is pretty disgusting.) Why not do what I do and make a panful at the weekend or one evening – it's not like making soup requires a lot of energy – then you've got a batch of zero-effort lunches to see you through the next few days?

As you'll see in this chapter, I'm a big fan of including grains and pulses in my soups, because it adds more texture (as well as goodness). For a little more oomph, I'll often top my soups (especially hot soups) with something crunchy, like toasted walnuts or sunflower seeds. Alternatively, you can just throw on some chunky croutons, or simply pair it with a chewy bread. Your soup, your rules.

And with many of these recipes, you can add whatever veg you have languishing in the fridge. Both the Bulgarian bean soup (see page 100) and the Warming winter soup (see page 105), for example, can easily accommodate extra veggies in the form of greens or roots, helping you to use up old produce and reduce food waste.

Yes, there are stock cubes; yes, there are powdered bouillons; and yes, making your own stock can be a faff, but it is technically easy, quicker than you think, and cannot be matched for flavour or nutrition. When boiling vegetables a lot of vitamins leak into the water, and a stock takes advantage of this, holding them in. Stock cubes are also often packed with MSG and palm oil, so, once again, making your own gives you more control over what you're putting into your body. A home-made stock really elevates a simple soup; I often use a bouillon for the heavy-hitting soups, but for subtle or fragrant soups a good stock is vital. You don't need to have all the ingredients listed below; this is a great way to use up any veg that's starting to go a bit limp. Having said that, I think this recipe gives a well-rounded flavoursome stock. I often add corn from the cob, lettuce, cucumber, leek or nettles, too. If you've got a pressure cooker or a slow cooker, this is even easier.

1 large onion

3 celery sticks

1 large carrot

2 big cabbage leaves

1 potato (100g/3½oz
    or the peel of 3 potatoes)

3 mushrooms

1 garlic clove

3 bay leaves

1 tsp black peppercorns

15g (½oz) fresh parsley

2cm (¾in) Parmesan rind
    (if you have any)

2 tsp salt

Staple vegetable stock

Roughly chop all the veg and put it into a large saucepan or stockpot. Add all the other ingredients plus 2 litres (3½ pints) of water and bring to a simmer. Turn down the heat to the lowest setting, put on a lid and leave to simmer gently for 1–2 hours.

Strain the stock through a sieve into a bowl and allow to cool before chilling or freezing in 500ml (16fl oz) portions. Stored in the freezer, this will keep for up to 3 months.

I know that a dahl is a dahl and not a soup, however, I like to eat the thinner, soupier versions by the bowl much like I do a soup. The magic of dahls are their simplicity, restrained mellow spicing and earthy natural flavours of split pulses. The burnt aubergine (eggplant) and the toasted white urid dahl provide a smoky twist, and if you want an extra lift you can stir through a teaspoon of garam masala right at the end. If you have a pressure cooker, you can speed everything up, but I don't mind letting mine simmer for an hour, providing a delicious perfume for my kitchen.

150g (5oz) split chana dahl

1 aubergine (eggplant)

1 medium onion, finely chopped

3 garlic cloves (2 in the initial mix, and 1 at the end), finely chopped

15g (½oz) fresh root ginger, peeled and chopped

1 red chilli

1 tsp salt

2 tsp ground turmeric

⅛ tsp bicarbonate of soda (baking soda)

20g (¾oz) white urid dahl

1 tsp cumin seeds

1 tsp mustard seeds

40g (1 tbsp) unsalted butter

15g (1 tbsp) fresh coriander (cilantro), stalks and leaves

Smoky dahl

Soak the chana dahl in a bowl of hot water for 30 minutes.

Hold the aubergine (eggplant) over a flame, or under a hot grill until the skin is black and its form has collapsed slightly. Turn it occasionally so it is burnt on all sides, this usually takes about 10 minutes. You want to ensure it is very smoky. Set aside, then, once cooled slightly, peel off the skin and tip the flesh into a bowl.

Drain the chana and put it into a medium saucepan. Add the onion, 2 of the garlic cloves, ginger and chilli to the pan. Add 2 litres (3½ pints) of boiling water along with the salt and turmeric, bring to a simmer, then turn down the heat and continue with a low simmer for 1 hour. After 40 minutes, add the bicarbonate of soda (baking soda) and mix through. You can add more water if you think the dahl is too thick.

Add the urid dahl, cumin seeds and mustard seeds to a dry frying pan and toast for about a minute until golden brown and the seeds pop, shaking the pan occasionally to prevent them burning. Add the butter and the final garlic clove and continue frying for 30 seconds. Immediately take this off the heat and stir it through the dahl.

Finely chop the coriander (cilantro), stir through the dahl and eat immediately. Stored in the freezer, this will keep for up to 3 months.

In Bulgaria a bean soup (bob chorba) is all about the beans. Bulgaria is known for its wide variety of beans and this soup made with a simple broth allows them to take centre stage. When I first tried bob chorba I was surprised by the flavours that come from herbs such as djodjen and summer savory. Djodjen is from the mint family and has a peppery spearmint flavour, which is what interested me most. For this book, I've gone for herbs that best mimic the flavours of the authentic versions. In this soup you can choose whatever beans you would like and it is nice to have a mix. Using a good home-made vegetable stock (see page 97) will really elevate this soup, as the broth is very simple.

10ml (¼fl oz) olive oil

1 medium onion, finely diced

1 carrot, finely diced

1 green (bell) pepper, deseeded and finely diced

1 small potato (about 100g/3½oz), finely diced

200ml (7fl oz) vegetable stock, shop-bought or homemade (see page 97)

½ x 400g (15oz) can chopped tomatoes

½ tsp salt

½ tsp ground black pepper

1 tsp paprika

15 fresh mint leaves, finely sliced

4 sprigs of fresh oregano (or ¼ tsp of dried)

250g (9oz) beans from a tin (drained weight), your choice, I like to go for a mix

Bulgarian bean soup

Heat the oil in a medium saucepan, add the onion and gently cook it for about 10 minutes until it is just soft but not coloured.

Add the carrot, pepper and potato to the pan along with the stock, chopped tomatoes, salt, pepper, paprika, mint leaves and oregano. Simmer for 25 minutes then add the beans. Simmer for a further 15 minutes, then serve, piping hot. Stored in the freezer, this will keep for up to 3 months.

If you are looking for a quick, nutritious and, most importantly, tasty soup this should be your go-to. There are seven different vegetables in this, as well as a hearty portion of lentils. It is hydrating but it is also a thick soup that feels substantial. The first part of this soup uses a base tomato sauce, which is also used in some of the meals in this book and is very versatile. When you make food from scratch you know exactly what is going into it; if you look at the label of a shop-bought tomato sauce you'll scan down a list of enhancers, emulsifiers and preservatives. This sauce is essentially just packed with vegetables, yet is so thick and tasty. I usually make three times the quantity so that I can have it to hand. You can make a very easy soup with this sauce using any two of your favourite vegetables, two of your favourite spices and 500ml (16fl oz) water.

serves 4

Base tomato sauce:

1 medium onion,
  finely chopped

20ml (¾fl oz) olive oil

1 small carrot, finely chopped

2 celery sticks, finely chopped

1 green (bell) pepper
  cheek, deseeded and
  finely chopped

1 x 400g (15oz) can
  chopped tomatoes

4 garlic cloves, minced

1 tsp salt

Soup:

10ml (¼fl oz) vegetable oil

1 medium onion,
  finely chopped

¼ butternut squash,
  peeled and chopped
  into 5mm (¼in) cubes

1 tsp ground cumin

¼ tsp ground cloves

¼ tsp ground black pepper

100g (3½oz) split red lentils

1 portion of Base tomato
  sauce (or 1 x 400g tin
  chopped tomatoes)

200ml (7fl oz) water

1 garlic clove, minced

Simple lentil soup
(and Base tomato sauce)

For the Base tomato sauce, sauté the onion in a medium saucepan with the olive oil until translucent (about 3 minutes).

Add the carrot, celery and green pepper to the pan and continue to fry gently for 5 minutes. Add the chopped tomatoes, garlic and salt. Pour in 200ml (7fl oz) water (half the volume of the chopped tomatoes' tin) and simmer for 20 minutes.

Blend until smooth (like really smooth). This can now be used for this soup, or stored in the fridge or freezer for another dish (see intro). Stored in the freezer, this will keep for up to 3 months.

For the soup, heat the oil in a medium saucepan and gently fry the onion for 5 minutes. Add the butternut squash cubes to the pan and cook for a further 3 minutes.

Add the spices and continue to cook for 1 minute before adding the lentils, Base tomato sauce and water, then bring to the boil and simmer for 10 minutes (add more water to get the soup to your desired consistency).

Add the garlic, stir through and simmer for another minute. Serve while still hot. Stored in the freezer, this will keep for up to 3 months.

Clockwise from left to right: Smoky dahl (see page 98), Warming winter soup (see page 105). Served with Sourdough loaf (see page 27) and Herby hit dressing (see page 139).

The best way to describe this soup is substantial. It is not a soup to be eaten with half a loaf of bread, it is a hearty and robust meal in itself. It is also a great way to kick-start a healthy diet, as it brings lots of fibrous veg and hydration and is very filling, keeping those hunger pangs at bay. It definitely veers towards a stew as opposed to a broth and is perfect to warm your cockles after a cold winter training run. I like to eat mine from a deep ceramic soup bowl.

1 medium onion,
  finely chopped

10ml (¼fl oz) sesame oil

1 medium carrot,
  finely chopped

2 celery sticks, finely chopped

2cm (¾in) fresh root ginger,
  peeled and finely chopped

600ml (1 pint) vegetable stock

1 x 400g (15oz) can
  chopped tomatoes

2 garlic cloves

½ tsp ground cinnamon

100g (3½oz) potatoes,
  peeled and chopped
  into 5mm (¼in) cubes

1 slice of stale sourdough

70g (3oz) frozen soya beans

2 tsp white miso

Warming winter soup

Put the onion in a medium saucepan with the sesame oil and gently fry for 10 minutes until softened, but not coloured. Add the carrot, celery and ginger to the pan and fry for a further 3 minutes. Add the stock, chopped tomatoes, garlic and cinnamon and bring to a simmer. Then toss in the potatoes and simmer for 15 minutes.

Cut the bread into 1cm (½in) pieces and add to the soup with the soya beans. Simmer for 3 minutes, then remove half a ladle of the liquid to a bowl. Dissolve the white miso into the reserved liquid, then return to the soup, stir through and remove from the heat.

Serve with a swirl of the Herby hit dressing (page 139). Stored in the freezer, this will keep for up to 3 months.

White miso

I've always loved sipping a small bowl of miso soup in Japanese restaurants, but I had no idea how versatile miso really is. So it was a revelation for me when I realised that a spoonful of white miso emulsified into a salad dressing provides a salty richness – which means you can reduce the fat content and still feel like you're eating something immensely satisfying.

I'm not exaggerating when I say white miso is one of those hero ingredients that has changed my cooking life. Creamy and salty and savoury (but not as savoury as red miso), white miso is a must in my kitchen.

What exactly is miso?

Miso is a fermented soybean paste that is made by inoculating trays of white rice with a kōji mould (or Aspergillus oryzae) and leaving it to ferment. Cooked soybeans and salt are then added and the mass is left to ferment, often for months, before being ground into a paste.

Miso originated in Ancient China, where it was called hishio. It was introduced to Japan in the seventh century by Buddhist monks, and was eaten by samurai or the wealthy aristocracy (because it was made from rice, which was only available for the wealthy).

How to use this hero ingredient

Miso comes in lots of different types, determined by where it is from, how long it is left to ferment and what other ingredients it may include. In this book I use a lot of white miso, which is the youngest of the miso family. I buy shiro miso, which is a rice and soybean paste that is fermented for six months. Once opened, it lasts for about three months in the fridge (although I leave mine for way longer). If you're visiting a Japanese shop, you may also find Saikyo miso, which is a sweeter white miso that needs to be consumed within a month. In general, when a recipe calls for white miso, don't be tempted to substitute it with red miso – it'll be too dominant.

White miso brings an umami depth to dishes, meaning it marries well with other earthy or salty flavours. It's also surprisingly good with sweet things. My whizzed mango dressing, for example, pairs white miso with mango to create a creamy dressing.

Miso does not dissolve easily, so it's best if you take a small amount of liquid from whatever you're preparing and use this to slacken the miso, before adding it to the main dish. So, for a broth, I'd dissolve the miso in a small cup of the broth before adding it to the pan. It's also best to add miso right at the end of the cooking process, because miso is a live, fermented food and boiling it will kill off the good micro-organisms.

You'll find white miso in my:

- Warming winter soup (see page 105)
- Heady garlic dressing (see page 139)
- Whizzed mango dressing (see page 136)
- Carrot and poppy seed almond cake (see page 181)
- Beet burgers and sweet tato buns (see page 168)

The Andalusian area of Spain boasts a host of fantastic regional cold soups, but the best known is gazpacho. This may seem like a simple soup, but balancing the flavours is a work of art. Too much garlic and it burns, not enough bread it becomes too thin, too much bread and it becomes turgid. My advice is to use good-quality vinegar and always keep tasting.

80g (3oz) stale white
   sourdough

1kg (2lb 4oz) ripe tomatoes,
   roughly chopped, or 1 litre
   (1¾ pints) tomato juice

1 red (bell) pepper, deseeded
   and roughly chopped

½ green (bell) pepper,
   deseeded and roughly
   chopped

½ cucumber (about
   120g/4½oz), peeled and
   roughly chopped, plus extra
   to serve

2 garlic cloves, minced

80ml (3fl oz) olive oil

20ml (¾fl oz) sherry vinegar

½ tsp ground cumin

1 tsp salt

Kimberley's gazpacho

Soak the bread in a bowl of water for 15 minutes to soften.

Add the tomatoes and peppers to a blender, along with the cucumber, garlic, oil, vinegar, cumin and salt, then finally squeeze the excess water out of the bread and add this too. Blend until really smooth (and I mean really smooth). Taste and see if it needs more salt, garlic or vinegar, then chill in the fridge until really cold.

Before serving, give it another blast in the blender, and add some extra water to slacken it if it is too thick.

Serve topped with chopped cucumber.

Salmorejo is like a stripped-down gazpacho, but it really highlights the concentrated tomato flavour. It is all about quality – don't make it without half-decent tomatoes, a fragrant olive oil and a good brand of sherry vinegar. It is surprisingly filling as a stand-alone soup.

800g (1lb 12oz) tomatoes
   (really good-quality ones)

3 tsp salt, plus extra to taste

1 garlic clove

250g (9oz) stale sourdough,
   torn into pieces

100ml (3½fl oz) olive oil

20ml (¾fl oz) sherry vinegar

Summer salmorejo

Put the whole tomatoes, salt, garlic and bread into a bowl and cover with 500ml (16fl oz) boiling water. Leave to sit for 1 hour.

Squeeze out the bread and place in a blender. Drain the tomatoes and garlic and save 200ml (7fl oz) of the liquid. Add the tomatoes, garlic and reserved liquid to the blender, along with the oil and vinegar and blend until smooth. Once you think you've blended enough, have a little taste, add more salt if required, then blend again until REALLY smooth.

Chill in the fridge until really cold, and stir through before serving.

Salad pick'n'mix

*how to feed your
body as well as
your imagination*

The humble green salad was first conceived by the Romans as raw leafy greens covered in a salty dressing. The name salad derives from the original Latin word *sal*, for salt, and even as this simple salad remains on menus today, it has been joined by countless dishes that are mesmerising in their complexity and variety. To some the word salad is synonymous with bland, watery and, dare we say it, 'healthy'. The same accusation is levelled at vegetarians by some meat eaters, and these labels often reveal more about those making the indictment and their lack of understanding on the subject. Salads can be a robust belly filler as well as fresh and light, and the healthy tag should be worn with pride.

Salads are a great way to steer your eating habits into a healthy direction. Not all salads are healthy – they can be swimming in a high-fat/high-sugar dressing, with 50 per cent mayonnaise or the majority as cheese, but as a concept salads are nutritious and they essentially give you a major dose of fresh vegetables and whole grains. I will eat a salad any time of the day, but they are most useful as a work lunch; easily transportable, fresh, energy giving, hydrating and full of fibre and nutrients.

This chapter introduces you to six base salads, six salad topper ideas and six tasty dressings that can be used in whatever combination you choose, and all will work perfectly in a lunchbox. They also come with tips for ways in which you can experiment and make them your own.

Sunday is a food-preparation day for me, and I like to make a big salad that will last me for the next three days. I have some really nice 500ml (16fl oz) wide-top bottles (I can't be doing with funnels), so I make bottlefuls of dressings at a time and basically rotate through the six I've listed here (forever making slight tweaks with new vinegars, spices, fruits, etc.). It is too easy to make a dressing with spoonfuls of sugar and loads of oil, but it is not necessary – you can make dressings thick and creamy by blending in avocado, sweet potato pulp, mango flesh or, my favourite, white miso, instead of oil. The biggest tip I can give is to only add dressings 5 minutes before you want to eat a salad (unless specifically stated). The acids in dressings break down cell structures in most vegetables and this can make a shredded, crunchy vegetable soft or crisp leaves limp.

Start with these six salads, toppers and dressings, then experiment and build your own versions. Have fun with it, you're winning if you pack them with different whole grains and a rainbow of fruits and vegetables.

Salad pick'n'mix

To build a salad, start with a base that is nutritious, filling and tasty. Next think about texture with a salad topper. You can then really pump up the flavour by adding a dressing. There are 6 bases, 6 toppers and 6 dressings in this book, which means you can make 216 different salads! Add your own favourites and your choices are endless . . .

choose your base

Roots and freekeh (see page 115)

Slaw is raw (see page 116)

Seedy tabbouleh (see page 118)

Lively salad (see page 119)

Gutsy salad (see page 121)

Dressed lentils (see page 124)

add some interest

Falafel bites (see page 125)

Seed clusters (see page 126)

Dukkah (see page 127)

Sprouted lentils (see page 130)

Lentil balls (see page 131)

Amaranth popcorn (see page 134)

bring it all to life

Goma dressing (see page 135)

Nouc mam cham (see page 135)

Tahini dressing (see page 136)

Whizzed mango dressing (see page 136)

Heady garlic dressing (see page 139)

Herby hit dressing (see page 139)

et voila – your chosen salad!

Seedy tabbouleh with lentil balls and a heady garlic dressing

I am a big fan of root vegetables in salads. The natural sugars caramelise while roasting and when they are cut up small they are like sweet tiny gems. For this salad I've used carrot, celeriac and sweet potato, but you can also use beetroot, swede or parsnip (they all need the 35 minutes of roasting, only the sweet potato roasts quickly). It is a good idea to introduce a variety of root vegetables into your diet as each has different indigestible starches, and this salad is a good way of doing that. It balances well with a sharp dressing such as the Herby hit dressing (see page 139) or becomes comfortingly warm if paired with the Goma or Heady garlic dressings (see pages 135 and 139). The crunchy salad toppers will give a textural dimension and nutty flavours complement the freekeh.

1 medium carrot (about 70g/2½oz), peeled and cut into 5mm (¼in) cubes

¼ celeriac (about 250g/9oz), peeled and cut into 5mm (¼in) cubes

10ml (¼fl oz) olive oil

1 sweet potato (about 150g/5oz), peeled and cut into 2cm (¾in) cubes

1 tsp fine salt

160g (5½oz) freekeh

300ml (10fl oz) vegetable stock

2 Little Gem lettuces

30g (1oz) raisins

[SALAD BASE]

Roots and freekeh

Preheat the oven to 180°C fan (200°C/400°F/gas mark 6).

Place the carrot and celeriac in a roasting tin, toss in the olive oil and roast for 20 minutes.

Remove the tin from the oven, add the sweet potato, sprinkle on the salt, shake it all around, then return to the oven for another 15 minutes.

While the vegetables are roasting, cook the freekeh. Simmer it in the vegetable stock for 15 minutes in a small saucepan with a tight-fitting lid on. Turn off the heat, leave the freekeh in the pan with the lid on for a further 5 minutes to absorb all the stock.

Mix the freekeh and roasted vegetables together in a large mixing bowl and leave to cool.

Once cooled, roughly chop the lettuce and toss through with the raisins.

To eat, simply toss through your favourite dressing. Once you've added the dressing it won't keep, though, so if you're making a big batch and eating portions for lunch throughout the week, make sure you only add dressing to the portion you are eating immediately. Stored in an airtight container in the fridge, this will keep for up to 3 days.

A great slaw is all about a good crunch. There are certain controversial elements to a slaw, but really it is just a question of your taste. For me personally, I'm not a fan of raw onion, but raisins are a must. Shop-bought coleslaw is often a cold, creamy soup, with cabbage and carrot suspended in a gelatinous gloop. I don't believe mayonnaise has to be present, but each to their own, and if you're using some, try a Japanese mayo. I like finely shredded, crisp veg and a zingy dressing. This slaw is particularly lifted by Seed clusters (see page 127) or Dukkah (see page 126). It is essential that whatever dressing you are using is added just 5 minutes before eating so that the acids take the edge off the cabbage, but not long enough for anything to go limp. When I lived in Malawi a cabbage salad was regularly served and the fineness of the shred was unreal. Since then I have always sharpened my knife before I prepare the cabbage and I go for as fine a shred as possible. Celery seeds are not 100 per cent necessary but I love the depth of flavour they bring and feel they give that final flourish to a well-rounded slaw.

2 small beetroot (about 120g/4½oz), peeled and chopped into batons

¼ sweetheart cabbage, finely shredded

2 carrots (about 200g/7oz), coarsely grated (you can choose whether to peel or not)

1 mango (works well from under-ripe through to ripe), peeled, stoned and sliced into strips

40g (1½oz) raisins

½ tsp caraway seeds

½ tsp celery seeds

[SALAD BASE]

Slaw is raw

Add the beetroot to a large mixing bowl with the cabbage, carrots and mango slices.

Throw in the raisins, caraway and celery seeds, toss all the ingredients together. Stored in an airtight container in the fridge, this will keep for up to 3 days.

To eat, simply toss through your favourite dressing. Once you've added the dressing it won't keep, though, so if you're making a big batch and eating portions for lunch throughout the week, make sure you only add dressing to the portion you are eating immediately.

serves 4

*Parsley, **much** like celery, so often sits behind other flavours as the enhancer, complement or base, grounding other flavours, but rarely as the stand-out taste. It is seldom the star of the show, but for tabbouleh you really must let parsley shine. I regularly take this salad to work for lunch **and** stuff it into toasted pitta with houmous, but it also goes really well with the Tahini, **Heady** garlic, Whizzed mango and Herby hit dressings (see pages 136–9). You can even keep it really simple with lemon juice, olive oil and salt. Tabbouleh is usually made with bulgur wheat, but this version includes amaranth and quinoa, as they provide all nine essential **amino** acids, giving you a comprehensive protein hit.*

40g (1½oz) amaranth seeds

40g (1½oz) quinoa

40g (1½oz) bulgur wheat

1 white onion, finely chopped

400g (14oz) tomatoes
(really nice ones),
deseeded and diced

1 tsp ground allspice

½ tsp ground cumin

2 bunches of parsley,
leaves and the half of
the stem near the leaves
(about 60g/2¼oz),
finely chopped

20g (¾oz) fresh mint leaves,
finely chopped

100g (3½oz) green olives,
stoned and sliced

[SALAD BASE]

Seedy tabbouleh

Put the amaranth and quinoa in a small saucepan and cover with 250ml (9fl oz) boiling water, then cook at a simmer for 6 minutes. Add the bulgur wheat and continue to simmer for 10 minutes. Take off the heat and allow to sit in the pan with the lid on for another 5 minutes to absorb all the liquid. Allow to cool.

Put the onion in a bowl and cover with cold water, then set aside for 15 minutes.

Add the tomatoes to a mixing bowl with the allspice and cumin, then stir through the herbs and olives. Drain the onion and add to the mix with the amaranth, quinoa and bulgur wheat.

To eat, simply toss through your favourite dressing. Once you've added the dressing it won't keep, though, so if you're making a big batch and eating portions for lunch throughout the week, make sure you only add dressing to the portion you are eating immediately. Stored in an airtight container in the fridge, this will keep for up to 3 days.

(See image on pages 128–129.)

Courgettes (zucchini) get a lot of negative press about being tasteless, slimy and pointless, but I think this is unfair. They are very versatile, providing moisture to cakes, a soft capsule for stuffing, a juicy building block for a ratatouille and, when marinated, a sponge to soak up dressing. This is my favourite way of eating courgettes and it makes up the bulk of this salad. Courgettes brown nicely when baked, then go really soft but keep their shape. They can then be steeped in a dressing and no one can say they are tasteless. If you grow courgettes you'll know that you get a bounty of fruit from a single plant, so finding recipes that use them is a must.

100g (3½oz) brown rice

2 courgettes (zucchini), about 400g (14oz)

20ml (¾fl oz) olive oil

Salt, for sprinkling

80g (3oz) green olives, stoned and sliced

50g (2oz) cornichons, sliced

½ cucumber, cut into 1cm (½in) chunks

50g (2oz) sesame seeds

[SALAD BASE]

Lively salad

Boil the rice in a pan with plenty of boiling water for 30 minutes, drain and set aside to cool.

Preheat the oven to 180°C fan (200°C/400°F/gas mark 6).

Slice the courgettes (zucchini) into rounds 5mm (¼in) thick. Brush with olive oil on both sides and place on a baking tray (if it's not non-stick you'll have to use baking parchment). Once you've filled two trays, sprinkle the courgettes with salt and roast in the oven for 35 minutes, or until golden brown. Once out of the oven, leave to cool.

Put the green olives and cornichons in a large mixing bowl with the cucumber chunks.

Toast the sesame seeds in a dry frying pan until just turning golden, then quickly tip them into the mixing bowl. Add the rice and courgettes and mix everything together.

Pour on the dressing at least 1 hour prior to eating and stir through to coat. Stored in an airtight container in the fridge, this will keep for up to 3 days.

Feeding our body isn't just about what can be absorbed through our small intestine, we want certain foods to pass right through and into our large intestine, feeding the trillions of micro-organisms that live there. I remember when wholewheat (wholegrain) pasta was brittle and chalky. My mum was a healthy-eating pioneer so we had it regularly, but as a child I longed for the chewier, soft texture of a heavily refined pasta. Nowadays wholewheat pasta has a great texture and most people wouldn't be able to tell the difference. This is a go-to salad for me when going to work. It stands up well to travelling and is very filling. It is also definitely a salad where you can sub in your favourites, or use what you have left over in the fridge, e.g. swap in chickpeas (garbanzo beans) for the haricot beans, sunflower seeds for pumpkin seeds, almonds for peanuts, and so on. This salad works very well with all the dressings, but I think the Goma dressing (see page 135) is the best match.

160g (5½oz) wholewheat (wholegrain) pasta

100g (3½oz) green beans, cut into 1cm (½in) pieces

30g (1oz) freekeh

30g (1oz) quinoa

100g (3½oz) mixed olives, stoned

1 x 400g (15oz) can haricot beans, drained

30g (1oz) pumpkin seeds

30g (1oz) roasted peanuts

[SALAD BASE]

Gutsy salad

In two saucepans bring some water to the boil. Cook the pasta in one according to the packet instructions until al dente. Once cooked, remove the pasta pieces with a slotted spoon and refresh in a bowl of cold water to quickly cool the pasta and stop it cooking further. Now add the green beans to the same pan of boiling water and simmer for 4 minutes. Once cooked, drain and refresh in a bowl of cold water to stop them cooking and to keep their colour.

In the second saucepan, simmer the freekeh for 4 minutes. Then add the quinoa and continue to simmer for a further 1 hour 10 minutes. Drain, refresh in a bowl of cold water, drain, and set aside.

In a large mixing bowl, combine the drained pasta and green beans with the freekeh, quinoa, olives and haricot beans.

Dry-fry the pumpkin seeds until they pop in the pan, then add them to the bowl with the other ingredients. Smash your peanuts in a pestle and mortar, add to the bowl and toss everything together.

Toss through your favourite dressing 20 minutes before eating. Stored in an airtight container in the fridge, this will keep for up to 3 days.

Quinoa and amaranth

People often refer to quinoa and amaranth as grains, but in fact they aren't grains. True grains come from grasses, while quinoa and amaranth are the seeds of non-grass crops, which technically makes them pseudocereals. But from a culinary and health point of view, we tend to slot pseudocereals in with other whole grains, like barley, brown rice and wholewheat products.

I wanted to include amaranth here because it hasn't yet found the foodie spotlight in the way that quinoa has. Amaranth is very similar to quinoa (it's a smaller seed, that's all), which means it's just as versatile as quinoa, just as useful in the kitchen, and just as good for you.

Ancient foods that still have so much to offer

Both plants originated in the Americas. Quinoa came from the Andean region of South America, while amaranth has a long history in central America, as well as the Andean region. Both were cultivated and used by ancient civilisations, including Mayans and Aztecs, and it wasn't until the arrival of the Spanish that these crops fell out of favour, being replaced by the cereals that we're more familiar with today, like wheat and maize.

Considering quinoa and amaranth are usually treated as carbs, they're great sources of protein (both contain all nine essential amino acids, making it a complete protein). Both are gluten free, and both are packed with fibre, making them friends to your microbiome. In other words, these tiny grains (seeds, whatever!) punch way above their weight.

How to use these hero ingredients

There are different types of quinoa and amaranth. White quinoa tends to cook quicker and has a lighter texture than red and black quinoa (which are crunchier, but arguably have a better flavour). With amaranth, you might get some darker seeds, but they tend to all have the same nutty, mild flavour. In the kitchen, it generally doesn't matter too much which type you use, so go with the variety you like best.

Quinoa and amaranth are incredibly versatile. They can be blended, popped, used raw as a crunchy crust, flaked to make a porridge, or (and this is the classic way) just simmered to create wonderful pearly seeds that give a gentle pop when eaten. You might also like to give millet a try – it's a grain (not a pseudocereal), but it can be used in a similar way to quinoa and amaranth, and is similarly high in protein.

You'll find quinoa and amaranth in my:

- THIS is granola (see page 44)
- Mum's Yorkshire parkin (see page 201)
- Banana chocolate muffins (see page 214)
- Seedy tabbouleh (see page 118)
- Beet burgers and sweet tato buns (see page 168)
- Amaranth popcorn (see page 134)

This robust salad can take a surprising amount of dressing. There is no need to massage the dressing into the kale — thankfully this is no longer a trend, but kale does soften nicely when steeped in an acidic dressing, unlike some other leafy greens. Kale is a nutrition booster that not only contains iron (as do all leafy greens), but it is also rich in vitamins A, K, B6 and C. It provides calcium, potassium and manganese, too, so it is serious at providing a salad health hit.

This salad works well with all the salad toppers and is particularly matched to the Heady garlic or Whizzed mango dressings (see pages 193 and 136). Actually, I like it with all the dressings.

100g (3½oz) Puy lentils (or any green/brown lentils)

225g (8oz) halloumi, cut into ½cm (¼in) slices

250g (9oz) kale (you choose the variety)

100g (3½oz) Kalamata olives, stoned and roughly chopped

2 chunky slices of stale sourdough

1 avocado

[BASE SALAD]

Dressed lentils

Simmer the Puy lentils in a pan filled with plenty of boiling water for 20 minutes until softened, drain and set aside.

Fry the halloumi in a non-stick frying pan until golden brown.

Wash the kale, then tear the leaves away from any tough stalks and discard them. Tear the leaves into pieces no bigger than 2cm x 2cm (¾in x ¾in) and place in a large bowl. Toss in the chopped olives.

Toast the slices of sourdough and cut into 5mm (¼in) cubes. Toss these into the bowl. Roughly chop the cooked halloumi and add to the mix along with the cooled Puy lentils. Finally, peel, stone and chop the avocado into 1cm (½in) chunks and gently fold this through the salad.

Toss through your favourite dressing 20 minutes before eating.

I'm not a 'sweet' or a 'savoury' person, but if a load of dishes were laid out on a table, I think I would go for falafel. I only like good falafel, though. I can eat a substandard scone, or a pappy bread roll, but falafel has to be crisp, moist and not at all stodgy. The main mistake people make is using canned chickpeas. Canned chickpeas are already cooked and therefore quickly become a paste (like houmous). Before you cook a falafel it needs a grainy consistency, which will become soft and crumbly once cooked. Dried chickpeas or fava beans remain quite hard when soaked, then when processed in the food processor will give you the perfect grainy texture.

130g (4½oz) dried chickpeas

1 garlic clove, minced

10g (¼oz) fresh coriander (cilantro)

10g (¼oz) fresh parsley

5g fresh mint

1 tsp ground coriander

1 tsp salt

½ tsp baking powder

20g (¾oz) plain (all-purpose) flour

2 tsp cumin seeds

10g (¼oz) black sesame seeds

10g (¼oz) white sesame seeds

Vegetable oil, for brushing

[SALAD TOPPER]

Falafel bites

Soak the chickpeas in a bowl of plenty of cold water for at least 12 hours. Drain and add to a food processor with the garlic, fresh herbs, ground coriander, salt, baking powder and flour. Pulse until grainy but not enough to make a paste. Transfer to a bowl, cover with beeswax or clingfilm and chill for 1 hour.

Toast the cumin seeds by dry-frying them in a pan for 2 minutes, then add to a bowl with the black and white sesame seeds.

Remove the chickpea mix from the fridge, then take 30g (1oz) of it and shape with wet hands into a ball or patty. Sprinkle with the seeds and place on a generously oiled baking tray. Continue with the rest of the mix, then brush the tops of the falafel with oil.

Preheat the oven to 170°C fan (190°C/375°F/gas mark 5). Leave the falafels to rest while the oven is heating up.

Bake for 25–30 minutes or until golden. Halfway through baking, flip the falafels then continue baking. These will keep for 3 days in an airtight container.

(See image on pages 132–133.)

How do you describe the bite of a toasted seed? Nuts give a heavy crunch, celery a crispy rasp, chilled chocolate a snap, but I would describe seeds as giving a delicate crackle. They are brilliant at giving a salad an extra texture and are jam-packed with goodness, each with their own balance of vitamins and minerals. Seeds also are a great source of fibre and contain monounsaturated fats. These are brilliant to store at work and can be snacked upon in their own right as well as used to top your lunchtime salad. Lots of recipes call for a mixture of syrup and oil to stick the seeds together, but I've found that most seeds become tacky when soaked, then when they are baked they glue to each other nicely.

70g (2½oz) sunflower seeds
30g (1oz) sesame seeds
30g (1oz) linseeds
10ml (¼floz) olive oil
10ml (¼fl oz) maple syrup
1 tsp soy sauce
½ tsp chilli powder
1 tsp fine salt

[SALAD TOPPER]

Seed clusters

Soak all the seeds in a bowl of cold water overnight.

The next day, preheat the oven to 150°C fan (170°C/325°F/gas mark 3), and drain the seeds in a sieve. Let them sit in the sieve for 5 minutes and every minute tap the side of it to release more excess liquid.

In a small bowl, combine the olive oil, maple syrup, soy sauce, chilli powder and salt. Add the seeds and toss until combined. Spread onto a lined baking sheet and bake for 25–30 minutes until golden brown.

Allow to cool completely then crumble into clusters and store in an airtight jar for up to a week.

(See image on pages 132–133.)

A table condiment exists to enhance a dish, but is a condiment a condiment if it is the star of the dish? Dukkah is an Egyptian spice mix that brings well-rounded, nutty, spicy, fragrant, smoky and toasted flavour notes all at once. Dukkah does not follow a set list of ingredients, and the flavour profile is very personalised. Below is a prized blend for my tastes but if you do your research you'll find over 50 different spices, nuts, herbs, grains that are used, so you can experiment and find your favourite flavour combination.

30g (1oz) salted
  roasted pistachios

30g (1oz) hazelnuts

30g (1oz) cashew nuts

20g (¾oz) sesame seeds

2 tsp coriander seeds

2 tsp cumin seeds

1 tsp nigella (black
  onion) seeds

1 tsp fennel seeds

1 tsp flaky sea salt

½ tsp paprika

¼ tsp ground turmeric

[SALAD TOPPER]

Dukkah

Shell the pistachios and set aside in a bowl.

In a dry frying pan, toast the hazelnuts and cashew nuts until golden brown, then add to the pistachios.

Put all the seeds into the now-empty pan and gently heat until the cumin seeds start popping, then transfer to a bowl.

In a food processor, pulse the nuts, salt, paprika and turmeric until coarse. Add the seeds and pulse twice, then transfer to an airtight jar. This will keep for up to 2 months, but the flavour is best if eaten within 2 weeks.

(See image on pages 132–133.)

Clockwise from left to right: Gutsy salad (see page 121), Amaranth popcorn (see page 134), Seed clusters (see page 126), Slaw is raw (see page 116), Seedy tabbouleh (see page 118) topped with Falafel bites (see page 125), Herby hit dressing (see page 139).

I remember getting into sprouting alfalfa for salads a decade ago, then I went through a phase of sprouting all kinds of grains and mulching them for breadmaking. Sprouting grains is really easy and provides another dimension in flavour, texture and health to your salads. A sprouted grain is a concentrated package of goodness and has more available nutrients than a mature grain. As the grain is germinating, starches are broken down, which increases nutrient content, and phytate is also reduced, which is an acid that stops us absorbing nutrients. You can sprout almost any grain using the same process but some are definitely easier than others. Green lentils are one of the easiest, so I've included them here as a starter, but you can have a go with whatever you choose (I've still not successfully sprouted fennel seeds but I'm going to keep trying). You can buy special sprouting equipment, but I just use a jar and a piece of muslin.

30g (1oz) dried green lentils

[SALAD TOPPER]

Sprouted lentils

Rinse your lentils in a sieve under a running tap until the water goes completely clear.

Add the lentils to a jar and fill it with water. Either soak them just before bed and leave them overnight, or soak them first thing in the morning and leave them immersed in water until the evening.

Pour off the water and attach some gauze or muslin to the top of the jar and fix with an elastic band. Leave the jar upside down on your draining board to allow excess water to drain away. You will need to rinse the lentils every 24 hours (and allow the water to drain again on your draining board) until you see the sprouts appearing.

I like to start eating the sprouted grains just as the sprout has appeared, but some people like to wait another day or two. Transfer to an airtight container and store in the fridge for up to 2 weeks.

(See image on pages 132–133.)

I've had lots of colleagues who decided to go vegetarian in the New Year but struggled when trying to replace the grilled chicken or flaked salmon that regularly topped their lunchtime salads. I brought in loads of these lentil balls and people loved them. The great thing is that once you've mastered the basic recipe there are countless ways in which they can be customised. I add all kinds of dried fruits, grains, seeds, flours and spices.

90g (3¼oz) cooked green lentils (or any other cooked grain you have)

100g (3½oz) firm tofu

100g (3½oz) sweet potato

50g (2oz) grated Cheddar cheese

20g (¾oz) plain (all-purpose) flour

½ tsp salt

1 tsp smoked paprika

½ tsp ground cinnamon

1 egg

30g (1oz) sesame seeds

[SALAD TOPPER]

Lentil balls

Put the lentils and tofu in a mixing bowl and mash these together with a fork. Finely grate the sweet potato and add this along with the cheese and mix.

Mix in the flour, salt, paprika, cinnamon and egg, then cover and chill in the fridge for 30 minutes. Pour the sesame seeds into a bowl and set aside.

Roll 20g (¾oz) portions into balls, then roll each in sesame seeds, place on a baking tray lined with baking parchment and chill in the fridge for 20 minutes.

Preheat the oven to 200°C fan (220°C/425°F/gas mark 7).

Bake for 20 minutes until golden. They can be eaten warm, or left to cool. Store in an airtight container for up to 3 days.

(See image on pages 132–133.)

Clockwise from left to right: Seed clusters (see page 126), Sprouted lentils (see page 130), Lentil balls (see page 131), Falafel bites (see page 125), Dukkah (see page 127), Amaranth popcorn (see page 134).

Salads are almost always about fresh flavours and crunchy textures. Amaranth seeds once popped like corn are fluffy and provide another dimension to a salad. These are subtly flavoured to give an umami and salty flavour. They're not designed to be the principal star of a dish, but to enhance or refine. They are best added to a salad just before eating and are easily stored in a jar.

100g (3½oz) amaranth seeds
1 tsp white miso
10ml (¼fl oz) maple syrup
10ml (¼fl oz) olive oil
¼ tsp salt
½ tsp smoked paprika

[SALAD TOPPER]

Amaranth popcorn

Put a large frying pan on the heat. Once hot, sprinkle in a few amaranth seeds; if they pop within 10 seconds the pan is hot enough; if they take longer, wait and try again in 1 minute. Once hot enough, pour in all the seeds and put on a lid. Shake the pan as the seeds pop. As soon as they have all popped, transfer them to a bowl.

In a separate mixing bowl, add all the other ingredients, stirring until smooth. Then tip in the popped amaranth and mix until coated. Allow to cool, then store in an airtight jar for up to 1 month.

(See image on pages 132–133.)

I love this dressing so much I often use it as a dip for my crudites. It also works well as a stir-fry sauce or spooned over a grilled fish. It doesn't last long in my fridge, that's for sure.

20g (¾oz) white
   sesame seeds
30ml (1fl oz) rice vinegar
10ml (¼fl oz) soy sauce
6 drops of Worcestershire
   sauce
10g (¼oz) white miso
20g (¾oz) tahini
20g (¾oz) toasted sesame oil

[SALAD DRESSING]

Goma dressing

Put all the ingredients into a jar and mix with a spoon until the miso is combined, then put on the lid and shake vigorously until smooth.

Store in the fridge for up to 2 weeks.

(See image on page 138.)

Salty, sweet, spicy, tangy, intense, the Vietnamese know how to liven up a dish with a simple dressing.

2 garlic cloves, minced
2cm (¾in) chunk of fresh
   root ginger, minced
25ml (1fl oz) lime or
   lemon juice
20ml (¾fl oz) rice wine
   vinegar
20ml (¾fl oz) fish sauce
2 tsp palm sugar (or
   soft brown sugar)
1 tsp salt
10ml (¼fl oz) sriracha

[SALAD DRESSING]

Nouc mam cham

Put all the ingredients into an airtight jar and shake to combine.

Store in the fridge for up to 2 weeks.

(See image on page 138.)

This is a fresh dressing packed full of herbs. The herbs and zing of the lemon are tempered and rounded out with the creamy tahini and white miso. It is a bold dressing and you can sub in whichever herbs you have in your fridge.

30g (1oz) light tahini

30ml (1fl oz) lemon juice

3g white miso

1 garlic clove, minced

1 tsp salt

5g fresh dill, finely chopped

5g fresh parsley, finely chopped

5g fresh coriander (cilantro), finely chopped

20ml (¾fl oz) warm water

[SALAD DRESSING]

Tahini dressing

Put the tahini, lemon juice, miso, garlic and salt into a jar. Press the miso with the back of a spoon until mixed in, then put on the lid and shake to combine.

Add the chopped herbs to the jar with the water before vigorously shaking again.

Store in the fridge for up to 2 weeks.

It was a revelation when I realised that blended mango is the perfect consistency for a dressing. All you need is some flavour balance and you have a wonderfully healthy option. If your mango is not nicely ripened, you may need to add a little honey.

90g (3¼oz) mango flesh

20ml (¾fl oz) white wine vinegar

1 tsp salt

1 garlic clove, minced

1 tsp white miso

[SALAD DRESSING]

Whizzed mango dressing

Put all the ingredients into a beaker and whizz with a stick blender until smooth. Transfer to an airtight jar.

Store in the fridge for up to a week.

(See image on page 138.)

Clockwise from top left to centre: Herby hit dressing (see page 139), Goma dressing (see page 135): Nouc mam cham (see page 135), Whizzed mango dressing (see page 136), Heady garlic dressing, (see page 139) Tahini dressing (see page 136).

This dressing stands up tall and demands to be taken seriously. Everything is big, but balanced. The sweet potato gives the dressing a glossy thickness without needing to load it with oil and sugar. I like to up the garlic, but this is up to you (and whoever you share a house with).

15g (½oz) white miso

1 garlic clove, minced

30g (1oz) puréed sweet potato

15g (½oz) wholegrain mustard

1 tsp salt

30ml (1fl oz) white wine vinegar

4 drops of Worcestershire sauce

10ml (¼fl oz) olive oil

15ml (½fl oz) water

[SALAD DRESSING]

Heady garlic dressing

Put all the ingredients into a jar and mix with a spoon until the miso is combined, then put on the lid and shake vigorously until smooth.

Store in the fridge for up to 2 weeks.

This dressing will make even the simplest salad sing. Avocado brings the velvet body to this dressing, and the herbs and spinach deliver an iron richness to give you a boost.

½ avocado, peeled and stoned

15g (½oz) fresh parsley, stalks and leaves

6g fresh coriander (cilantro), stalks and leaves

3g fresh basil leaves

25g (1oz) spinach leaves

10ml (¼fl oz) olive oil

1 tsp white wine vinegar

Zest of 1 lemon

20ml (¾fl oz) lemon juice

½ tsp salt

[SALAD DRESSING]

Herby hit dressing

Put all the ingredients into a beaker and whizz with a stick blender until smooth. Transfer to an airtight jar.

Store in the fridge for up to a week.

Salad pick'n'mix

Fresh and filling

*meals to inspire
and nourish*

When I was growing up, dinner – or 'tea' as we called it, being from Yorkshire – was the most important meal of the day. Without fail we would all eat together every evening at 6pm, all seven of us crammed around the table, enjoying a shared meal and catching up on the day's events. Sadly, this habit of always eating dinner at roughly the same time, sat at the table, isn't something I've managed to carry forth into my adult life – at least, not consistently. But wherever possible, I like to make a nutritious meal from scratch every day. I just might be eating it at 5 o'clock, or 8 o'clock, on the sofa, or wherever.

Like most people, I have my easy fallback recipes, things I can cook quickly after a long day at work. Then there are more special meals that require a little extra time or effort, which are usually reserved for the weekends. (Although, saying that, I might turn to these more time-consuming recipes on a weeknight when I need to decompress after a tough day. For me, time in the kitchen is a good way to de-stress. I find chopping, stirring, kneading and rolling all very meditative.)

This chapter is a rundown of my favourite dinner (or tea!) choices. These are the recipes I rotate over and over again. With these favourites, I know I'm getting a healthy balance of whole grains, vegetables, pulses and fats, but, equally important, I'm eating something delicious. It's much easier to maintain a healthy lifestyle when you actually enjoy what you're eating. When every dinner feels like a punishment, you'll be reaching for the takeaway app in no time. You want food that's good for you, and good to eat.

So, with that mantra in mind, this chapter gives you healthy, delicious meals to suit whatever you're in the mood for. Want something fresh and vibrant? Check out my Zamboanga prawns (see page 147) or Kosambari (see page 146) tortilla fillings. Need a speedy fix? I recommend the Quick bean squashy chilli (see page 161) or Tangy aubergine and blue cheese pasta (see page 167). Fancy a warm, hugging bowlful of food? You can't go wrong with my simple Pasta bake (see page 151). And if you're after an impressive centrepiece, how about Roasted bream (see page 173) or Banitsa (a traditional Bulgarian pastry that looks every bit as good as it tastes, see page 166). There's a balance of staple dinners for every night of the week and ideas for special occasions, so all your bases are covered. Enjoy . . .

The higher the hydration for tortillas (the more water you add to the dough), the fluffier and more bubbly they are. The dough will be very sticky at first and as you get used to handling it, you can add another 10ml (¼fl oz) of water. Then you can add more. Often tortillas are neutral in flavour and wrap around a tasty filling. Here are three ways to boost the flavour of the tortillas themselves for no extra effort, and pack them with the goodness of seeds, nuts and herbs.

makes 6 tortillas

225g (8oz) plain (all-purpose) flour, plus extra for dusting

50g (2oz) wholemeal plain (whole-wheat all-purpose) flour

1 tsp baking powder

½ tsp salt

50g (2oz) natural yogurt

100ml (3½fl oz) warm water

20ml (¾fl oz) vegetable oil

Glorious tortillas

Put the flours, baking powder and salt in a mixing bowl. Mix the yogurt, water and oil in a jug. Pour over the dry ingredients and mix together to form a dough. Knead for a minute in the bowl until smooth, then cover and leave for 15 minutes.

Knead for 1 minute in the bowl, then leave again for 45 minutes.

Divide the dough into 6 pieces and roll each piece out into 10cm (4in) circles. Leave on a flour-dusted surface, then continue rolling each out to 20cm (8in) – the tortillas are very elastic and it is easiest to roll them when allowing them to relax.

Heat a heavy frying pan or baking stone to a medium-high heat. Dry-fry each tortilla for about 1 minute on each side. The tortilla should really puff up with lots of big bubbles within 10–20 seconds of hitting the pan. If not, you may need to increase the heat.

Keep the tortillas wrapped in a clean tea towel until ready to eat. This will keep them soft.

Alternatives

- *Whizz 10g (¼oz) fresh coriander (cilantro) – stalks and leaves – and 5g (⅛oz) fresh basil leaves with the yogurt, water and oil to give herby tortillas that are bright green in colour.*

- *Add 4 tsp of Dukkah (see page 127) to the flour and baking powder. This is my favourite way to boost the flavour of tortillas.*

- *Add 1 tsp turmeric, ½ tsp nigella (black onion) seeds, ½ tsp mustard seeds to get bright yellow spicy tortillas.*

Fresh and filling

Salmon is such a versatile fish. It is not too 'fishy' for those who prefer the milder fish tastes, it is oily and moist so stands up to all kinds of cooking, it is meaty yet delicately flaky, pretty in pink and doesn't have lots of fine bones. Best of all, it is packed with omega 3 fatty acids, potassium, selenium, a plethora of vitamins and is a great source of protein! There are a million recipes out there for simple spicy salmon and almost all of them work well. Here is my version that uses gochujang paste, which brings umami sweetness to the spicy.

300g (10½oz) skinless
   salmon fillets

1 tsp gochujang paste

10ml (¼fl oz) honey

5ml (1 tsp) soy sauce

1 garlic clove, minced

5ml (1 tsp) toasted sesame oil

½ tsp salt

6 tortillas (bought or
   home-made, page 143)

Extras:

2 Little Gem lettuce,
   finely shredded

Quick crunchy pickles
   (see page 239) or ¼
   cucumber, finely sliced

Sour cream or Silken
   cucumber dip (see page 90)

Sticky spicy salmon

Prepare the salmon by ensuring it is dry (use some kitchen paper if you've washed it).

Mix the gochujang paste, honey, soy sauce and garlic in a flat bowl. Add the salmon. Ensure the salmon fillets are coated then cover and leave to marinate in the fridge for at least 1 hour, or up to 3 hours. If you're really short of time it will still be tasty if you marinate for 10 minutes, however.

Heat a non-stick frying pan to medium-hot and grease with the sesame oil. Add the salt to the salmon. Place the fillets in the pan and fry for 3 minutes on one side, then turn down the heat to medium and cook for another 3–4 minutes on the other side. Allow to stand for 5 minutes.

Meanwhile, in a clean pan, fry the tortillas, one at a time, for about 10 seconds on each side. Fill the tortillas with the salmon and any of the extras you like, then wrap and eat!

This tortilla wrap gives you and your microbiome a mighty boost! In this crunchy Indian salad there is a wealth of indigestible starches, providing your gut bacteria with a feast. The crisp crunch is balanced with the smooth bean tapenade and the omelette (wrap within a wrap) provides substance. I make this for friends who want to switch to a healthier diet but are under the misconception that healthy food is bland. This recipe packs in the flavour and textures and is also a fun dish to make together.

Kosambari:

50g (2oz) split yellow
    mung beans

50g (2oz) cucumber, chopped
    into 5mm (¼in) cubes

50g (2oz) carrot, finely grated

50g (2oz) fresh coconut,
    finely grated

6 tortillas (bought or
    home-made, page 143)

Juice of 1 lime

1 tsp salt

20ml (¾fl oz) vegetable oil

1 tsp mustard seeds

1 tsp fennel seeds

¼ tsp asafoetida

10g (¼oz) fresh coriander
    (cilantro), stalks and leaves

Bean tapenade:

1 x 400g (15oz) can
    black beans, drained

50g (2oz) Kalamata
    olives, stoned

1 tsp dried oregano

½ tsp paprika

10ml (¼fl oz) olive oil

1 garlic clove, minced

1 tsp red wine vinegar

Omelettes:

Vegetable oil, for greasing

6 eggs

½ tsp salt per egg

Kosambari plus

Soak the mung beans in a bowl of cold water for 1 hour.

To make the bean tapenade, put half the beans with all the other ingredients into a food processor (reserving the remaining beans for the omelette) and pulse until smooth, but not too paste-like. I prefer it to retain a bit of texture. Set this aside in a bowl.

Add the cucumber cubes to a mixing bowl with the grated carrot and coconut. If you're using store-bought tortillas, I would fry my tortillas at this time – dry-fry in a frying pan, one at a time, for about 10 seconds on each side.

Drain the mung beans in a sieve and rinse under cold running water. Knock the sieve well to ensure all the water drains away, then add the mung beans to the mixing bowl. Add the lime juice and salt and mix through. In a small frying pan, heat the oil on a medium heat, then add the mustard and fennel seeds. Once the mustard seeds pop, remove from the heat and stir through the asafoetida for 20 seconds, then pour this onto the salad and mix through.

Wipe clean the pan and return to the heat with 1 teaspoon of oil. Whisk the first egg in a bowl with ½ teaspoon of salt, pour into the frying pan and swirl around to make sure it's thin. Sprinkle with some of the reserved black beans and allow to cook for 1 minute before transferring to a plate. Continue with the rest of the eggs and beans.

To eat, take a tortilla, spread some tapenade down the middle, line with an omelette, fill with the kosambari and sprinkle with the coriander (cilantro). Wrap and eat!

My friend Regie introduced me to this sauce from her city in the south of the Philippines, and I don't know anyone whose face has not lit up on tasting it. She told me that the sauce doesn't have a specific name and is referred to simply as 'Zamboanga-style coconut milk sauce'. I've shortened this to just name her home city! You can make the sauce ahead of time and do it in a bigger batch. I make four times the amount and freeze portions until I need them. You can use this much like a curry paste for all kinds of saucy dishes. The rich creaminess of the sauce contrasts with the crunch of the shredded cabbage and peanuts.

10ml (¼fl oz) vegetable oil

400g (14oz) raw king prawns, shelled

6 tortillas (bought or home-made, page 143)

½ tsp salt

Juice of ½ lemon

¼ sweetheart cabbage, very finely shredded

100g (3½oz) salted peanuts

Zamboanga sauce:

1 onion, finely chopped

1 tsp vegetable oil

1 x 400g (15oz) can coconut milk

4 garlic cloves, minced

1cm (½in) piece of fresh root ginger

15g (½oz) peanut butter

1 tsp annatto powder (or paprika)

1 tsp salt

Zamboanga prawns

First make the sauce. Add the onion to a medium saucepan with the vegetable oil and fry gently for 5 minutes. Add all the other ingredients and bring to a simmer. Cook for 10–15 minutes until the sauce is thick.

Bring a frying pan to a high heat, add the vegetable oil, followed by the prawns. Cook for 2 minutes on one side, then flip and cook for a further minute on the other side. Turn the heat to the lowest setting and add the Zamboanga sauce.

Meanwhile, if you're using store-bought tortillas, fry the tortillas in a clean pan, one at a time, for about 10 seconds on each side.

Add the salt and lemon juice to the cabbage in a bowl and toss to combine, then fill your tortillas with the cabbage, prawns and a good sprinkling of peanuts. Wrap and eat!

Clockwise left to right: Glorious tortillas (see page 143) with Sticky spicy salmon (see page 144), Quick crunchy pickles (see page 239), Glorious tortillas with Zamboanga prawns (see page 147).

This is a once-a-week recipe for me. I change my vegetables depending on what is available in my kitchen and what is in season. I've added cheese to this one as I presume I'll have comments galore if a caramelised layer of cheese is not present on a pasta bake, but I often make this without cheese and love the crispy top of the pasta and vegetables. This is a simple and humble recipe and a great shout for anyone who is carb-loading.

2 fennel bulbs, cut into
   1cm (½in) slices

1 large head of broccoli
   (about 300g/10oz florets),
   florets separated

10ml (¼fl oz) olive oil

½ tsp salt

400g (14oz) pasta

1 portion of Base tomato
   sauce (see page 101)

150g (5oz) mixed
   olives, stoned

100g (3½oz) mature
   Cheddar, grated

Herby oil:

1 green chilli

1 garlic clove, minced

30ml (1fl oz) olive oil

10ml (¼fl oz) white
   wine vinegar

½ tsp salt

Fresh parsley

Fresh basil

Simple pasta bake

Preheat the oven to 200°C fan (220°C/425°F/gas mark 7).

Put the fennel bulbs and the broccoli florets into a large mixing bowl with the olive oil and salt and toss so that everything is covered. Set the bowl aside for later.

Prepare a large baking tray with baking parchment. Add the fennel and roast for 20 minutes, then add the broccoli and roast for a further 20 minutes.

With 10 minutes left on the timer, prepare the pasta. Cook it according to the packet instructions, but reduce the cooking time by one-third. You want the pasta to be slightly undercooked so that it will continue to cook while baking. Drain and add to the large mixing bowl with the tomato sauce and 100ml (3½fl oz) of water. Add the roasted veg and olives, then toss everything together. Transfer this to a large baking dish, top with the grated cheese and bake for 20–25 minutes depending on how crispy you want the top.

Make the herby oil by adding all the ingredients to a food processor and pulsing until you have a coarse mix.

Once out of the oven, allow the pasta bake to sit for 5 minutes before drizzling with the herby oil and serving.

These Vietnamese pancakes are a great idea if you need to make a gluten-free meal and depending on what dressing you use can be vegan too. I usually make the batter in the morning (it doesn't take long at all) and then keep it in the fridge until you need it later in the day. Bánh Xèo translates as 'sizzling pancakes', and they're meant to be on the thin side, meaning that this is a really healthy choice: heavy on the veg, light on the stodge. You really can fill it with whatever you like. This crunchy veg gives a good base, but you can add a protein or stuff with condiments and pickles.

Pancakes:

200g (7oz) rice flour

20g (¾oz) cornflour (cornstarch)

1 tsp ground turmeric

250ml (9fl oz) coconut milk

½ tsp salt

250ml (9fl oz) water

Vegetable oil, for frying

Salad:

1 small red onion, finely sliced

1 carrot, coarsely grated

½ cucumber, cut into batons

1 mango, peeled, stoned and sliced

3 spring onions (scallions), sliced on the diagonal

20g (¾oz) fresh mint leaves, shredded

40g (1½oz) fresh coriander (cilantro), leaves and stalks, shredded

30g (1oz) roasted salted peanuts

Nouc mam cham or Goma dressing (see page 135)

10g (¼oz) black sesame seeds

Bánh xèo with crunchy veg

Put all the pancake ingredients except the oil into a blender and blend until smooth. Leave to sit for 30 minutes.

Meanwhile, start on the salad. Put the sliced red onion in a bowl of cold water. Add the carrot to a large mixing bowl with the cucumber, mango, spring onions (scallions), mint and coriander (cilantro). Drain the onions and add to the bowl, tossing everything to combine. Smash the peanuts with a pestle and mortar and set aside.

Heat a frying pan on a high heat with 2 teaspoons of vegetable oil. Pour in a thin layer of the batter (it will have loads of little bubbles), put on a lid, and fry for 2 minutes until the edges just start going brown. Slide onto a plate and continue until you've finished the batter, adding more oil as needed.

Dress the salad with the dressing. To eat, pile a portion of salad onto a pancake, sprinkle with the peanuts and sesame seeds, fold over and eat with your hands or cutlery – your choice!

This Chinese pancake is all about textures! Delightfully crisp on the outside with laminated, moist, chewy layers inside, it is similar to the parathas of India and is really easy to make. Now when you hear the word laminated, please do not think of the deceptively tricky croissants or puff pastry that take hours (days) to prepare, the texture of these flatbreads simply comes from thinly rolled-out dough brushed with oil and concertinaed to produce the layers. This is a favourite dinner in our house and is definitely an impressive, fresh and healthy dish if you're having people over.

250g (9oz) plain (all-purpose) flour

50g (2oz) wholemeal plan (whole-wheat all-purpose) flour

5g poppy seeds

200ml (7fl oz) boiling water

Pancake filling:

20ml (¾fl oz) toasted sesame oil

3 tsp plain (all-purpose) flour

4 spring onions (scallions), finely chopped

Flaky sea salt, for sprinkling

Vegetable oil, for rolling and frying

Salad:

1 small red onion, finely sliced

1 carrot, coarsely grated

½ cucumber, cut into batons

1 mango, peeled, stoned and sliced

3 spring onions (scallions), sliced on the diagonal

20g (¾oz) fresh mint leaves, shredded

40g (1½oz) fresh coriander (cilantro), leaves and stalks, shredded

30g (1oz) roasted salted peanuts

Nouc mam cham or Goma dressing (see page 135)

10g (¼oz) black sesame seeds

Cong you bing

First make the pancakes. Toss the flours and poppy seeds in a heatproof mixing bowl, pour over the boiling water and stir with a wooden spoon until it creates a sticky dough. Cover and leave for 5 minutes.

Knead the dough inside the bowl for 3 minutes. Do not add any further flour at this stage. If you have a stand mixer you can mix with a dough hook for 5 minutes. Divide into 4 pieces, set on a baking tray, cover and leave for 30 minutes.

Meanwhile, start on the salad. Put the sliced red onion in a bowl of cold water. Add the carrot to a large mixing bowl with the cucumber, mango, spring onions (scallions), mint and coriander (cilantro). Drain the onions and add to the bowl, tossing everything to combine. Smash the peanuts with a pestle and mortar and set aside.

Mix the sesame oil and flour for the filling in a bowl and set aside. Take the first piece of dough and roll it out on a lightly oiled surface to about 30cm x 30cm (12in x 12in). Brush with the oil mixture and sprinkle the spring onions (scallions) and flaky salt over the surface. Concertina-fold the dough, then coil into an ammonite shape and set aside while you do the same with the remaining 3 pieces of dough.

Take the first ammonite and roll out a disc about 25cm (10in) in diameter.

Heat a frying pan on a medium heat with 1 teaspoon of vegetable oil. Fry the pancake for 3 minutes on one side, flip and fry for another 3 minutes on the other side. Set aside and continue with the remaining 3 pancakes.

Dress the salad with the dressing, add this to the pancakes, and sprinkle with the peanuts and sesame seeds. Fold in half and serve.

Various forms of stuffed cabbage leaves are part of many different food cultures. In Bulgaria, pickled cabbage leaves filled with rice and meat called sarmi are baked for hours in a gyuveche, a traditional earthenware pot. Sarmi are serious comfort food, but it's the pickled cabbage leaves that really intrigued me as this brings in another layer of flavour. This recipe uses the same pickling liquor as the Pickled poached vegetables (see page 84), which can be saved and used multiple times between the two recipes.

Poaching liquor:

500ml (16fl oz) water

100ml (3½fl oz) white wine vinegar

100ml (3½fl oz) lemon juice

3 bay leaves

2 celery sticks, roughly chopped

1 green (bell) pepper cheek, roughly chopped

20g (¾oz) fresh parsley

1 tsp salt

Parcels:

1 Savoy cabbage

1 medium onion, finely chopped

20ml (¾fl oz) vegetable oil

2 tsp ground cumin

1 tsp black pepper

1 carrot (about 100g/3½oz), coarsely grated

1 parsnip (about 150g/5oz), coarsely grated

1 red (bell) pepper, deseeded and coarsely grated

200g (7oz) jasmine rice

1 garlic clove, minced

1 tsp salt

700ml (1¼ pints) vegetable stock (add 500ml/16fl oz, then 200ml/7fl oz)

Slaw:

70g (2½oz) Savoy cabbage, very finely sliced

30ml (1fl oz) of your chosen salad dressing

Pickled cabbage parcels

Put all the liquor ingredients in a medium saucepan on a medium heat and simmer for 10 minutes. Take the 12 biggest leaves from the cabbage, then cut them in half, removing the central stem, and poach in the simmering liquor for 5 minutes.

Gently fry the onion in a pan on a low heat in the vegetable oil for 5 minutes. Add the cumin and black pepper and fry for a further minute. Add the carrot, parsnip and pepper to the pan and continue to gently fry for 5 minutes. Add the rice, garlic, 500ml (16fl oz) of the stock and the salt, cover with a lid and simmer for 10 minutes. The rice will not be cooked through, but this is okay. Allow to cool for 10 minutes.

Take a pickled cabbage leaf and spoon in a dessertspoon of the rice mixture (about 25g/1oz). Roll up halfway, fold in the sides and continue rolling up. Place this in a frying pan that has a lid, or a large saucepan. Continue with the parcels until you've used all the leaves and the base of the pan is filled. Pour over the remaining stock, place a heavy plate on top and put on the lowest heat of your hob for 30 minutes.

Once the cabbage parcels are ready, toss the shredded cabbage with your preferred dressing and serve on top of the parcels.

This recipe is a fusion dish that needs to be eaten. Fish finger sandwiches are a guilty pleasure of mine, and I'm a fan of shop-bought frozen fish fingers, served with some crusty white bread and tomato ketchup. This sandwich, however, is on another level. Focaccia is the perfect bread for a sandwich – stretchy, billowy and with a crust that crackles. This version is mildly spiced so that the fish still sings and works very well with a sweet and tangy sauce.

100g (3½oz) panko
  breadcrumbs

250g (9oz) hake fillets

1 egg

20g (¾oz) plain
  (all-purpose) flour

1 tsp Dijon mustard

1 tsp paprika

½ tsp salt

Spicy focaccia (see
  page 160), to serve

Focaccia fish finger sandwich

Preheat the oven to 180°C fan (200°C/400°F/gas mark 6).

Spread the breadcrumbs onto a baking sheet and toast in the oven
for 5 minutes.

Prepare the fish, making sure it is very dry (pat with kitchen paper if
not fully dry). Cut into fish finger pieces (remember, they will shrink by
about 20 per cent when cooked). Mix the egg, flour, mustard, paprika
and salt together in a bowl, dip one of the fish pieces in until coated,
then roll in the breadcrumbs straight away and place on a baking tray,
spaced apart. Continue until you have completed all the fish fingers,
then bake for 15 minutes.

Serve piled in your spicy focaccia sandwich with tomato ketchup,
mango chutney or mayonnaise. If you want an extra pickle kick,
serve with my Tangy carrot chutney (see page 241).

Sponge:

300g (10oz) strong
    white bread flour
500ml (16fl oz) warm water
10g (¼oz) instant yeast

Dough:

350g (12oz) strong
    white bread flour
2 tsp ground turmeric
2 tsp cumin seeds
2 tsp nigella (black
    onion) seeds
2 tsp salt

Marinade:

2 tsp garam masala
Juice of 1 lemon
2 tsp fennel seeds
40ml (1¼fl oz) vegetable oil,
    plus extra for greasing

How to make the spicy focaccia

Mix the sponge ingredients together in a bowl until it looks a bit like a porridge consistency, then leave, covered, in a warm place for 30 minutes.

The sponge mixture should be bubbly and active, ready to be made into the dough. Add the bread flour and turmeric, and mix in a mixer with a dough hook for 10 minutes (alternatively, you can mix with your hands in the bowl, but it will be a very sticky mixture at this stage). Bash the cumin seeds in a pestle and mortar and add to the dough along with the black onion seeds and salt. Continue to mix for 3 minutes.

Place the dough in a lightly oiled large bowl, cover, and allow to prove until at least doubled in size, about 1 hour. Halfway through proving, stretch the dough by wetting your hands, sliding them down the side of the dough, lifting the bottom and folding over the top (do this stretching 6 times, turning the bowl as you go).

Preheat the oven to 200°C fan (220°C/425°F/gas mark 7).

Combine all the marinade ingredients in a bowl. Transfer the dough to a well-oiled baking tray (about 40cm x 25cm/16in x 10in) and brush with the marinade. Leave now until doubled in size (about 45 minutes) and periodically prod the surface of the dough with your fingers to create indentations.

Bake for 30 minutes. At 10 minutes, 20 minutes and 25 minutes into the baking time, remove from the oven and brush with the marinade.

Once baked, slide onto a wire rack to cool. This is best eaten on the same day, but toasts nicely the following day.

For some, a chilli is purely about a rich, almost muddy sauce, simmering for an age with butter, red wine, chicken livers or cocoa powder. For others it's more of a thin but fiery soup eaten with cornbread. I enjoy a thick bold sauce but I like to keep a tomatoey freshness. A chilli is a great way to get a wide variety of vegetables into one meal, and with the protein and fibre added through the beans, it would be hard to find a healthier meal. Robust, smoky flavours match well with sweetness and the roasted squash provides a natural candied intensity that adds further depth. I like to pile loads of salsa on top as I love the clash of hot and cold, spicy and sharp, sweet and sour.

20ml (¾oz) olive oil

500g (1lb 2oz) butternut squash, chopped into 5mm (¼in) cubes (skin on)

½ tsp salt

1 portion of Base tomato sauce (see page 101)

2 tsp chipotle paste

1 tsp smoked paprika

1 tsp ground cumin

½ tsp chilli flakes

3 star anise

200g (7oz) jasmine rice

2 x 400g (15oz) cans mixed beans, drained

50g (2oz) spinach

Salsa:

100g (3½oz) cherry tomatoes

100g (3½oz) melon (your choice)

100g (3½oz) cucumber

½ avocado, peeled and stoned

½ tsp white miso

1 garlic clove

½ tsp salt

Juice of 1 lime

a few fresh mint leaves

Quick bean squashy chilli

Preheat the oven to 200°C fan (220°C/425°F/gas mark 7).

Drizzle the olive oil onto a baking tray, toss the squash in the oil, sprinkle with the salt and roast for 40 minutes.

While the squash is roasting, put the tomato sauce into a medium saucepan with the chipotle paste, smoked paprika, cumin, chilli and star anise and bring to a simmer for 25 minutes.

While the sauce is simmering and the squash is roasting, it is time to make the salsa. Chop the tomatoes, melon and cucumber into small cubes. Mash the avocado with the miso, garlic, salt and lime juice. Finely shred the mint leaves and mix everything together.

Put the rice in a saucepan, pour on boiling water 1.5cm (⅝in) above the level of the rice, bring to a simmer, put on a tight-fitting lid and turn the heat to the lowest setting for 15 minutes.

Remove the star anise, add the beans and spinach and continue to simmer for 5–10 minutes until the squash is ready, then add this to the saucepan with the spinach and simmer for a further minute.

Serve the chilli atop a bowl of rice with a generous serving of salsa. Stored in the freezer, this will keep for up to 3 months.

(See images overleaf.)

*Quick bean
squashy chilli
(see page 161).*

Butternut squash

When I look at the hero foods I turn to time and time again, butternut squash is right up there. It's one of those easy-going, versatile vegetables that should make you cheer every time you see it in your veg box.

Lots of pumpkins are a bit floury and wet (it's important to pick the right variety), but butternut squash never lets me down. With its smooth, dense flesh — that can be roasted, grated, blended, you name it — butternut squash is a wonder ingredient for satiating those rich, sweet, hearty cravings. Perfect for taking a healthy dish from meh to mmmm.

It was the sweetness that drew me in...

When we think of indulgent, feel-good foods, we're often thinking of smooth or sweet sensations – basically, things that rely on cream, butter and sugar. Squash can hit that sweet, smooth and creamy spot perfectly, making it a great stand-in for less virtuous ingredients. Perhaps that's one of the reasons why squash is so adaptable, why it's just as comfortable starring in a vegetarian main course as it is playing the supporting role in a moist cake.

Squash also happens to be ridiculously good for you, being rich in vitamins A and C, potassium and fibre. And it can stand up to heavy spices and strong flavours like a pro, making it impossible to get bored of (and believe me, I've tried).

How to use this hero ingredient

Whenever a recipe doesn't call for a whole butternut squash, don't be tempted to leave the leftover squash languishing in the fridge (where, despite your best intentions, you know you'll leave it for ages before finally chucking it on the compost). Use it. Throw it in a hot oven for 45 minutes or so, scoop out the flesh, then add a can of coconut milk, a crushed garlic clove, your favourite spice mix and blend to a smooth soup. (Surprisingly, this is just as good cold, with smashed cucumber, in the summer.)

Or, if you don't even have the energy to clean your blender (me, most Wednesday evenings), simply rub a garlic clove over a slice of sourdough toast, spread on a generous layer of the roasted flesh, crumble blue cheese on top and sprinkle with seeds (or my favourite, Dukkah – see page 127), and that's dinner sorted. For my weekday lunches, I top a salad with roasted cubes of squash (skin on, yes, it works), some grains, seeds and a zingy dressing. Beats limp lettuce and fridge-cold tomatoes any day!

You'll also find butternut squash in my:

- Simple lentil soup (see page 101)
- Quick bean squashy chilli (see page 161)
- Simnel cake bites (see page 182)
- Plum upside-down frangipane (see page 219)

This is for people who fancy a challenge and doing something new. I love quick recipes, but I also love spending time deep in a process, learning new skills. Banitsa is a pastry from Bulgaria with almost identical cousins in neighbouring countries, such as Turkey, where it is called Borek. It is crispy on the outside and delightfully soft on the inside. I was taught how to make the pastry the traditional way, stretching it over the backs of your hands, but rolling with a pin also works well, as you want it thin. If you want to cheat, you can use sheets of filo pastry. I love eating this with houmous and an array of pickles.

1 egg

175ml (6fl oz) warm water

200g (7oz) strong white bread flour, plus extra for dusting

160g (5¾oz) plain (all-purpose) flour

60ml (2¼fl oz) olive oil

nigella (black onion) seeds and sesame seeds, to sprinkle on top

Filling:

1 egg

100g (3½oz) Sirene cheese (or you can use feta)

10g (¼oz) chopped fresh dill

10g (¼oz) chopped fresh tarragon

¼ tsp salt

Banitsa

Whisk the egg and the water together in a mixing bowl, then add the flours to form a sticky dough. Leave this to rest at room temperature for at least an hour.

Turn out onto a floured surface and knead for 30 seconds. Divide into 2 pieces and make each piece into a ball. Now flatten out the ball and the idea is to gently manipulate the dough so that it stretches to a long oblong about 60cm (24in) across. The traditional way to do this is to let it hang down from the backs of your hands as you keep switching it from one hand to another (I always start with a rolling pin). You can simply lift it just off the table and pull it around, or you can use a rolling pin, if you prefer. You may get some small tears, but this is okay.

Preheat the oven to 180°C fan (200°C/400°F/gas mark 6).

Lay the first oblong down on a floured surface and brush with some of the olive oil. Make the second dough oblong, then place this on top and brush it with oil.

Mix the egg, cheese, herbs and salt in a bowl and sprinkle this across the pastry. Roll it into a long sausage, divide into 4 and then coil each into a swirl onto a lined baking sheet. Brush with oil and sprinkle with the seeds, then bake for 30 minutes until they are golden and crispy.

This is best eaten fresh, but can be stored in an airtight container for up to 1 day.

This might not be a combination of flavours and textures you're used to, but it really works. Aubergines (eggplants) become silky and marry well with spaghetti when steamed. Balsamic vinegar and capers cut through to provide a tangy lift and Kalamata olives and blue cheese give depth and richness.

300g (10oz) cherry tomatoes

20ml (¾fl oz) olive oil

2 aubergines (eggplants), cut into 2cm (¾in) chunks

400g (14oz) spaghetti

30ml (1fl oz) balsamic vinegar

3 garlic cloves, minced

100g (3½oz) Kalamata olives, stoned

40g (1½oz) capers

30g (1oz) fresh basil, torn

120g (4½oz) blue cheese

Salt, for sprinkling

Tangy aubergine and blue cheese pasta

Preheat the oven to 200°C fan (220°C/425°F/gas mark 7).

Put the tomatoes in a roasting tray with the olive oil and season with salt. Roast for 20 minutes, or until soft and charred.

Sprinkle the aubergines (eggplants) with ½ teaspoon of salt. Set a steamer over a pan of boiling water on a medium heat, add the aubergines, put the lid on and steam for 20 minutes.

Put the spaghetti in a large saucepan with plenty of boiling water and cook according to the packet instructions (make sure you don't overcook).

While the spaghetti is cooking, put the roasted tomatoes (plus juices) into a large frying pan on a medium heat. Add the balsamic vinegar, garlic, olives and capers and stir through. After 5 minutes, add a ladle of water from the pasta saucepan, turn up the heat and add the steamed aubergines.

Drain the spaghetti and add to the frying pan, along with the basil, blue cheese and more seasoning if required. Stir everything around gently until coated and transfer to pasta plates to serve.

I've had so many mushy, pasty veggie burgers in my time, which is very annoying as a good burger is a thing of beauty. Beans are really good, but they are the biggest culprit for that pasty texture. You need to make sure the mix isn't too wet. The great thing about burgers is that you can make loads ahead of time and freeze them, especially for the barbecue season. At some point the brioche bun became synonymous with the premium burger. A sweet and soft bap to compliment a juicy burger, crisp gherkins and a tangy sauce makes complete sense, however, the clandestine addition of sugar to food traditionally free from it has been pervasive and is not necessary. Brioche is not innocently sweet and soft – look at a recipe and you'll find it's enriched with butter, sugar and eggs. These burger buns are very similar to a traditional brioche bun, but the dough has no added sugar, butter or egg, giving you a bun that tastes indulgent yet is healthier. It might be difficult to imagine until you've tried one, but the heavy, earthy sweet potato actually makes these rolls incredibly soft, fluffy and golden. And they're not just for burgers . . .

Beet burgers and sweet tato buns

Burgers:

250g (9oz) canned black beans, drained

100g (3½oz) cooked beetroot, finely chopped

80g (3oz) prunes, finely chopped

100g (3½oz) grated Cheddar, finely grated

80g (3oz) sweet potato, peeled and finely grated

4 garlic cloves, finely grated

150g (5oz) sourdough breadcrumbs

2 tsp white miso

2 tsp Dijon mustard

1 tsp smoked paprika

1 large egg

2 tsp fine salt

10g fresh flat-leaf parsley, finely chopped

40g (1½oz) quinoa

8 Sweet tato buns (see page 171) or shop-bought burger buns

Preheat the oven to 180°C fan (200°C/400°F/gas mark 6).

Put the black beans onto a baking tray and bake for 15 minutes to dry them out. Add these to a mixing bowl, allow to cool slightly, then squeeze with your hands a few times until they are slightly mushed but you can still easily tell they are beans.

Add the beetroot and prunes to the mix, along with the cheese, sweet potato, garlic and breadcrumbs.

In a small bowl, whisk the miso, mustard, smoked paprika, egg and salt with a fork until smooth. Add this to the mixing bowl with the parsley, then mush the whole thing together until it is all combined. Shape the mix into 8 burgers, each 1cm (½in) thick. Sprinkle the quinoa onto a plate and press the burgers into this on both sides to give a crunchy crust. Chill in the fridge for at least 1 hour or until ready to cook.

To cook, bake in the oven for 10 minutes, then fry for 6 minutes on each side in a frying pan on a medium heat, then 1 minute on each side on a high heat to get a good char. Alternatively, grill on a barbecue for 6 minutes on each side. Serve in the sweet tato buns with your choice of condiments.

How to make the Sweet tato buns

260g (9oz) sweet potatoes

20ml (¾fl oz) light olive oil, plus extra for greasing

1 tsp salt

2 tsp instant yeast

140ml (5fl oz) warm water

340g (12oz) strong white bread flour

60g (2oz) strong wholemeal (whole-wheat) bread flour

1 medium egg

Black sesame seeds, for sprinkling on top

Preheat the oven to 180°C fan (200°C/400°F/gas mark 6).

Start by roasting the sweet potatoes in their skin for 40 minutes. Once cooled, peel and blend until smooth. This can be done ahead of time; I freeze this as portions so I can defrost when needed.

Mix the sweet potato pulp, oil, salt, yeast and warm water, then add the flours and bring together to form a dough (this is a sticky dough). Cover with beeswax wrap or clingfilm and leave to rest for 10 minutes.

Now you have to gently knead for 5 minutes. I prefer to do this in the bowl and just use a spatula. You are not really kneading so much as stretching the dough. If you have a stand mixer and a dough hook it is a lot easier. Cover and leave in a warm place to rise until doubled in size (about 1 hour).

Knock back the dough and divide into 8 pieces. Form these into tight balls and transfer to a lined baking sheet (spaced well apart, about 5cm/2in).

Cover with oiled cling film and leave until at least doubled in size (about 1 hour, but don't worry if it's longer, definitely make sure they've doubled in size). At this time, preheat the oven to 200°C fan (220°C/425°F/ gas mark 7).

Beat the egg, then gently brush the egg wash on the buns and sprinkle with the sesame seeds before baking for 12–14 minutes.

Allow to cool before slicing with a serrated knife. These are best eaten fresh, but are good the next day toasted.

I love eating food with my hands, and if you are going to use your hands as utensils, this is a good way to start as it is pretty clean. Roasting a whole fish is the easiest way to cook it and provides a great communal eating experience. Sea bream is a surprisingly robust, quite fatty fish that stays moist during roasting and works well with a pickle. The pickle in this recipe is not sharp, as the vinegar is heavily balanced out with the natural sweetness of the grapes, pepper, fennel and carrot. It is a great sharing dish that leaves you feeling both refreshed and indulged.

Pickle:

1 yellow (bell) pepper, deseeded and finely sliced

1 tsp fennel seeds

40g (1½oz) caster (superfine) sugar

80ml (3fl oz) white wine vinegar

100ml (3½fl oz) water

¼ tsp salt

125g (4½oz) red grapes, cut in half

1 small carrot (about 70g/2½oz), coarsely grated

1 garlic clove, minced

Fish:

900g (2lb) sea bream

1 tsp salt

1 lemon

Extras:

250g (9oz) brown rice

2 romaine lettuce hearts

100g (3½oz) salted roasted peanuts

Roasted bream dream

Add the yellow pepper to a small saucepan with the fennel seeds, sugar, vinegar, water and salt. Simmer on a medium heat for 15 minutes. While this is simmering, add the grapes, carrot and garlic to a heatproof bowl. Pour over the peppers and cooking liquor and leave to stand while you prepare everything else.

Put the brown rice into a medium saucepan, cover with 500ml (16fl oz) of boiling water and simmer for 30 minutes with a lid on. Once cooked, put aside with the lid on for at least 10 minutes (or until you're ready to eat).

While the rice is cooking, prepare the fish. Preheat the oven to 190°C fan (210°C/425°F/gas mark 7).

Wash the fish and make a single incision lengthways along the spine on both sides, then place in a baking dish. (The incisions mean it is easier to eat the flesh later.) Sprinkle the skin liberally with salt, then slice the lemon, add 4 slices into the cavity and place the rest on top of the fish. Pour 200ml (7fl oz) of boiling water into the dish, then bake for 18 minutes.

While the fish is baking, cut off the base of the lettuces, pull apart the leaves, keeping them intact, and put on a plate. Crush the peanuts using a pestle and mortar (not too much, just so that they break in half) and transfer to a bowl.

To eat, take a piece of lettuce and fill with some rice and fish, spoon over some of the pickle and liquor, sprinkle with peanuts and enjoy!

Cacio e pepe is a very popular Italian pasta dish, beautiful in its simplicity. It is cheesy, creamy and rich. My sister-in-law made this one evening alongside bruschetta and realised that the bruschetta topping perfectly complemented the cacio e pepe. The clash and contrast of rich and fresh is a delight and is my go-to quick summer meal. Since the cheese brings salt to the pasta, I don't add salt to the salsa, however, a generous sprinkle of flaky salt on serving lifts the tomatoes. This meal is all about the preparation, get everything ready and you're going to make it work.

400g (14oz) really good
   tomatoes, deseeded and
   cut into ½cm (¼in) cubes

5ml (1 tsp) sherry vinegar

2 garlic cloves, minced

3g fresh basil

10ml (¼fl oz) olive oil

5ml (1 tsp) lemon juice

2 tsp black peppercorns

500g (16oz) spaghetti

60g (2oz) pecorino,
   finely grated

Flaky sea salt, to taste

Summer salsa spaghetti

Mix the tomatoes in a bowl with the vinegar, garlic, basil, oil and lemon juice.

Crush the peppercorns to a coarse powder and set aside.

Cook the spaghetti according to the packet instructions in a medium saucepan. Halfway through, remove 50ml (2fl oz) of the cooking water.

Once the spaghetti is cooked, drain in a colander and leave to the side. Put the cheese and pepper into a mixing bowl, pour in 25ml (1fl oz) of the cooking water and whisk until the cheese has melted and the sauce is thick. Add the rest of the water and keep whisking. Throw in the spaghetti, then toss around so that all the spaghetti is coated in the cheese mixture.

Serve the spaghetti topped with the tomato salsa and flaky sea salt to taste.

Sweet somethings

*have your (home-baked)
cake and eat it*

While I love a traditional cake, I must admit I like sweet yeasty breads and buns just as much. Possibly even more. (Is it because you can apply an extra layer of something tasty, like jam or chocolate spread, on top or in the middle? Perhaps. Or maybe it's just because I'm a bread-baker at heart.)

That's why you'll find a few bready treats in this chapter, like Saffron hot cross-less buns (see opposite) and Kozunak (Bulgarian Easter bread that's baked as a loaf, see page 192). But if you're a cake person, I've still got you covered with show-off cakes such as Carrot and poppyseed almond cake (see page 181) or Vegan coffee cake (see page 186). Then there are individual beauties, like my Pistachio and grapefruit financiers (see page 185) or Simnel cake bites (see page 182), which look lovely arranged on a plate for your friends to help themselves to.

Ordinarily, a cake is made with butter (or oil), sugar, flour and eggs. If you watched *Bake Off*, however, you'll know I have a habit of reducing the fat and sugar and replacing them with more nutritious ingredients – where possible, that is. So you won't be surprised to see I do the same thing with these recipes. I don't want to give any spoilers, but there are some pretty unexpected ingredients in this chapter. Bear with me, though. Because while these methods may seem unconventional, you'll still get the same delicious results – without the post-cake guilt that more indulgent bakes can trigger. Yes, I know we shouldn't be labelling any food as bad or naughty. It's just food. But, personally, I don't feel amazing after eating a slice of cake that's laden with sugar or fat, and I think many people would agree. (We may feel good while we're eating it. But afterwards, not so much. Especially when there are another eight slices left on the cake stand, just waiting to be eaten...) My point is, this chapter is about getting nothing but pleasure from your sweet somethings. Isn't that why we turn to cake in the first place?

But let's forget the 'is cake naughty or nice?' debate and focus on the really important issue: should you have your cake with a cup of tea or a cup of coffee? I like mine with a cup of coffee (incidentally, coffee is full of polyphenols that feed your microbiome – sorry, I can't help myself). Tea or coffee, you'll be spoilt for choice on which cake or bun to have alongside.

I love hot cross buns, the soft, spicy, yeasty buns studded with dried fruit and coated in a sticky glaze, but we can definitely leave off the crosses. If you love tradition, or you have a religious faith and like the symbolism, pipe them on, but I'm more than happy to ditch them and here's why – the crosses are a flour and water solution that bakes chewy and tough and spoils the soft bite of the freshly baked bread. Hot cross buns are as much about aroma as they are about flavour, and this recipe provides a heady mix of both. Shop-bought hot cross buns have become very stodgy, almost doughy, and cannot be eaten untoasted, and they often have as much sugar and butter as a whole cake. The dried fruit is enough to bring the sweetness, and, in my opinion, butter should be spread onto the bun after toasting. Sweet yeasted breads that contain a lot of dried fruits provide a sweet hit, while dispensing loads of vitamins, minerals and fibre.

280ml (9½fl oz) warm water

Pinch of saffron threads

10 drops of orange oil
   or the zest of 1 orange

300g (10oz) strong white
   bread flour, plus extra
   for dusting

180g (6oz) strong wholemeal
   (whole-wheat) bread flour

7g (¼oz) instant yeast

1 tsp salt

1 tsp ground cardamom

½ tsp grated nutmeg

50g (2oz) soft prunes,
   quartered

80g (3oz) raisins

50g (2oz) candied peel

Oil, for greasing

Glaze:

1 tsp ground cinnamon
50ml (2fl oz) water
50g (2oz) soft brown sugar
1 tsp malt extract

Saffron hot cross-less buns

Put the warm water in a jug and add the saffron threads and orange oil.

In a mixing bowl, combine the flours, yeast, salt, spices and prunes. Pour in the water and bring together to form a shaggy dough. Cover and allow to sit for 10 minutes. Knead for 1 minute in the bowl and as you do this the prunes should break up and streak through the dough. Cover with beeswax cloth or clingfilm and leave to prove for 30 minutes in a warm place.

Add the raisins and the candied peel and gently knead for 1 minute to distribute the fruit. Cover and leave to rest for 10 minutes.

Turn out onto a lightly floured surface, divide into 9 pieces and roll into tight balls. Place these on a lined baking tray (1cm/½in apart if you want them touching, or 3cm/1¼in apart for distinct buns). Cover with an oiled piece of cling film and leave to rise until doubled in size (about 1 hour).

Preheat the oven to 200°C fan (220°C/425°F/gas mark 7).

Once the buns have doubled in size, bake for 12 minutes.

As the buns are cooling slightly, it's time to make the glaze. In a small saucepan, simmer the glaze ingredients on a medium heat until thick and sticky. Brush on the baked buns and allow to cool before eating.

These are best eaten freshly baked, but stored in an airtight container will last up to 3 days and are great toasted.

This is a take on one of my favourite cakes from my childhood. My mum was uber healthy and our cakes were regularly packed full of seeds, ground nuts and vegetables, so it always seems strange to me that we continue to make cakes that only contain fats, sugar, eggs and highly refined flours. These cakes satiate the need for a treat, but why not have a delicious cake and know that lots of the ingredients are helping to fuel your body in a good way, too? This cake is sweet, delicious, full of mighty nutrients and has an umami depth that comes from the miso. It will also guarantee that you'll have seeds in your teeth all day. You're welcome!

20g (¾oz) chia seeds

30g (1oz) poppy seeds

80ml (3fl oz) milk

1½ tsp white miso

1 large egg

90g (3¼oz) caster (superfine) sugar

Zest of 1 lemon

50ml (2fl oz) olive oil, plus extra for greasing

1 tsp almond extract

100g (3½oz) plain (all-purpose) flour, plus extra for dusting

1 tsp baking powder

30g (1oz) ground almonds

1 small carrot (about 100g/3½oz), finely grated

To decorate:

100g (3½oz) icing (confectioners') sugar

Juice of the zested lemon

20ml (¾fl oz) liquid glucose (available in most big supermarkets)

Flaked (slivered) almonds, for scattering

Carrot and poppy seed almond cake

Put the chia and poppy seeds, milk and white miso into a small saucepan on a medium-high heat and bring to the boil. As soon as it reaches temperature, take it off the heat.

Preheat the oven to 160°C fan (180°C/350°F/gas mark 4) and grease and flour a small bundt tin (about 20cm/8in).

In a large mixing bowl, whisk the egg and sugar until light and creamy and doubled in volume (this can take up to 10 minutes). Continue whisking while adding the lemon zest, olive oil and almond extract. Then mix in the seed and milk mix.

In another bowl, combine the flour, baking powder and ground almonds, then fold this through the wet mix. Finally, gently mix through the carrot and transfer everything to the tin. Bake for 30–35 minutes or until a skewer inserted in the middle of the cake comes out clean.

While the cake is baking, put the icing (confectioners') sugar, 3 teaspoons of lemon juice and the liquid glucose into a small jar and shake it until mixed. The icing should not be too thick as you want it to run off the cake, so add more lemon juice if required – but be careful, just do a bit at a time as it soon becomes too slack. Toast the flaked almonds in a dry frying pan until golden, shaking the pan to prevent them burning, then immediately transfer to a bowl and set aside.

Once the cake is out of the oven, pour over any lemon juice remaining. Allow the cake to cool in the tin for 5 minutes, then turn out onto a wire rack set over some baking parchment. Pour over the icing so that it runs down the sides of the cake and sprinkle over the toasted almonds.

This is not a traditional Simnel cake, but my version on the theme. Essentially it's a light fruit cake straining under the weight of marzipan. The sponge is made healthier by having no fats and instead uses grated butternut squash to provide a light and moist crumb. The fragranced flavours of cardamom and orange are rounded out softly by the dark rum and sugars.

I am shocked by the portion sizes of cake slices in coffee shops and cafes nowadays. Let's start a new fashion of cake bites; the most enjoyment comes in the first couple of mouthfuls, and there is nothing stopping you having more if you want.

150g (5oz) soft brown sugar

40g (1¼oz) malt extract

3 large eggs, separated

75g (3oz) dried apricots, roughly chopped

75g (3oz) prunes, roughly chopped

75g (3oz) raisins

150g (5oz) finely grated butternut squash

15 drops of orange oil (or zest of 1 orange)

75ml (3fl oz) dark rum

150g (5½oz) plain (all-purpose) flour

75g (3oz) ground almonds

1½ tsp baking powder

Pinch of salt

1½ tsp ground cardamom

Almond marzipan:

30g (1oz) soft brown sugar

1 egg yolk

1 tsp liquid glucose

1 tsp almond extract

30g (1oz) icing (confectioners') sugar

70g (2½oz) ground almonds

Simnel cake bites

For the marzipan, whisk together the brown sugar, egg yolk, glucose and almond extract in a small saucepan. Heat gently on a low heat and whisk continuously until pale and hot (about 5 minutes).

Put the icing (confectioners') sugar and ground almonds into a large, heatproof mixing bowl, pour in the hot sugar mix and stir to combine until it forms a dough, then wrap in cling film and place in the fridge while you make the cake.

Preheat the oven to 170°C fan (190°C/375°F/gas mark 5). Line a 20cm (8in) loaf tin with baking parchment and set aside.

Beat together the sugar, malt extract and egg yolks in a large mixing bowl for a few minutes until pale and creamy. Add the apricots and prunes to another large mixing bowl along with the raisins. Mix in the squash with the orange oil and rum.

Combine the flour, ground almonds, baking powder, salt and cardamom in a bowl, then fold into the wet mix.

Beat the egg whites in a clean bowl until they hold soft peaks. Fold this gently into the cake batter. Transfer to the lined tin and bake for 50 minutes, or until a skewer inserted in the middle of the cake comes out clean.

Remove from the oven and leave to cool. Once the cake has cooled, trim off the top to make it flat, roll out two-thirds of the marzipan and use it to cover the top of the cake. Slice the cake into 15 pieces using a sharp knife. With the rest of the marzipan make balls or shapes to place on top of each cake bite, and if you want to toast them, simply use a blowtorch or place under a hot grill until lightly golden.

I don't often do fancy bakes, but if I want fancy, I go financier fancy. Financiers are named for their resemblance to gold bars and in my opinion they are so good they could be used for currency. The cake delights with its contrasts – rich and robust earthiness through the beurre noisette and ground nuts balanced perfectly with the delicacy of a surprisingly light structure and zingy grapefruit. Burning butter (beurre noisette) is an easy technique to bring a richer buttery flavour. Heating the butter separates the butterfat from the milk solids, and these solids begin to brown, but once you get an amber golden colour you need to remove from the heat to avoid it becoming a beurre noir! You don't need to put pink colouring in the icing, but I think it makes these cakes look so pretty and financiers deserve a glow-up.

60g (2oz) unsalted butter, plus extra for greasing

1 pink grapefruit

100g (3½oz) icing (confectioners') sugar

30g (1oz) plain (all-purpose) flour, plus extra for dusting

20g (¾oz) wholemeal plain (whole-wheat all-purpose) flour

½ tsp baking powder

40g (1½oz) unsalted pistachio nuts, whizzed to the texture of ground almonds (100g/3½oz once shelled is just over 40g/1½oz)

3 large egg whites

2 tsp orange blossom water

Topping:

85g (3oz) icing (confectioners') sugar

15ml (½fl oz) grapefruit juice (from above)

10g (¼oz) liquid glucose

Pink food colouring

Flaked (slivered) pistachios, to decorate

Pistachio and grapefruit financiers

Brown the butter by placing it in a small saucepan on a medium heat until it foams (about 5 minutes). Allow it to cook until golden brown, then remove from the heat and leave until cool, but not set.

Zest the grapefruit and add this to a mixing bowl with the icing (confectioners') sugar, flours, baking powder and ground pistachios. Toss all these together, then beat in the egg whites and orange blossom water. Stir through the browned butter then cover and chill for 1 hour.

Preheat the oven to 170°C fan (190°C/375°F/gas mark 5). Grease your chosen tin with butter and dust with flour. Fill the tin three-quarters full with the batter, then bake for 20 minutes or until a skewer comes out clean. Leave in the tin for 5 minutes, then transfer to a wire rack to cool.

Beat the icing (confectioners') sugar, grapefruit juice and liquid glucose with enough pink food colouring to give it a blush. Pour half over the financiers, allow to set, then pour over the rest and sprinkle with the pistachios.

Stored in an airtight container, these cakes keep nicely up to three days.

This cake has been developed from a vegan recipe I always use that's by Dan Lepard, my go-to baking guru. I don't like it when vegan recipes are a poor relative of their rich dairy cousins, and this cake is a stand-alone champion. It deserves to be made not as a vegan version of a cake, but simply as an amazing cake. The prunes, water and oil emulsify together to create a solution that mimics the properties that usually come from eggs, while also providing a healthy hit of fibre and vitamins. The extra gluten in bread flour also helps with the structure, sweet potato gives major moistness, and the vinegar gives the raising agent a boost. Coffee is an earthy flavour and it goes well with the nutty sweetness of the halva. Halva is a sesame-based sweet from the Middle East that manages to be both dense and strangely fluffy. It comes in lots of different flavours; the nutty versions, as well as honey and chocolate, would go perfectly with this recipe.

Vegan coffee layer cake

10g (¼oz) instant coffee granules

100g (3½oz) prunes

150ml (5fl oz) light olive oil

1 tsp red wine vinegar

10g (3½oz) malt extract

2 tsp vanilla extract

140g (5oz) caster (superfine) sugar

100g (3½oz) finely grated sweet potato

125g (4½oz) strong white bread flour

50g (2oz) plain (all-purpose) flour

1 tsp ground cinnamon

2 tsp baking powder

1 tsp bicarbonate of soda (baking soda)

100g (3½oz) halva, plus extra to decorate (optional)

Icing:

1 tsp instant coffee granules, plus extra to decorate

100g (3½oz) silken tofu

1 tsp vanilla extract

150g (5oz) icing (confectioners') sugar

In a heatproof jug, dissolve the instant coffee granules in 200ml (7fl oz) boiling water, then add the prunes and leave for 5 minutes.

Grease and line three 20cm (8in) round cake tins and preheat the oven to 170°C fan (190°C/375°F/gas mark 5).

Put the prune mixture in a blender with the oil, vinegar, malt extract and vanilla and blend until smooth. Pour the blender contents into a large mixing bowl and stir through the sugar and grated sweet potato. Add the flours, cinnamon, baking powder and bicarbonate of soda (baking soda), and beat to a thick batter. Divide between the 3 tins and crumble the halva evenly on top of them.

Bake for 20 minutes (or until a skewer inserted in the middle of the cake comes out clean), then remove from the tin and transfer to a wire rack to cool.

While the cake cools, make the icing. Add a few drops of boiling water to the coffee granules in a bowl and stir just until they've dissolved. Blend this together with the silken tofu and vanilla extract. Gently combine this with the icing (confectioners') sugar, cover and chill in the fridge for 30 minutes, then into the freezer for 20 minutes. If the icing is too thin, put back in the freezer until it reaches the desired consistency.

Once the sponges are completely cooled, layer them together with the tofu icing. Top with the icing, then sprinkle a few more coffee granules, and more halva, if desired.

Kozunak plait (see page 192) served with butter and raspberry jam.

Getting the perfect iced bun isn't easy. It is not just about getting maximum fluff to the crumb, you want a degree of stretch and chew. Growing up in my small town, Botham's bakery made the best lemon buns — soft round buns studded with raisins and topped with a lemon icing. This recipe is my homage to my hometown bun. I've used the Chinese tang zhoung method of adding gelatinised starches to the mix by making a roux with the water and some of the flour. This swells the starch and allows it to hold more liquid, therefore increasing overall hydration, which ensures a soft crumb. Sweet potato pulp adds sweetness and moistness without needing any extra fat or sugar.

100ml (3½fl oz) warm water

200g (7oz) strong white bread flour

130g (4½oz) sweet potatoes, roasted and blended to a purée

10ml (¼fl oz) light olive oil

½ tsp salt

1 tsp instant yeast

1 tsp caraway seeds

Zest of 1 lemon

80g (3oz) raisins

Icing:

10ml (¼fl oz) lemon juice

100g (3½oz) icing (confectioners') sugar

10ml (¼fl oz) liquid glucose

Iced lemony buns

Mix the warm water with 20g (¾oz) of the flour in a small saucepan. Heat gently until the mixture becomes a thick roux, stirring constantly (this should take about 1 minute). Set this aside until cooled.

Mix the sweet potato purée, oil, salt and yeast into the roux, then add the remaining flour, caraway seeds and lemon zest and bring together to form a dough (this is a sticky dough). Cover with beeswax wrap or cling film and leave to rest for 10 minutes.

Now you have to gently knead for 1 minute. I prefer to do this in the bowl and just use a spatula. You are not really kneading so much as stretching the dough. If you have a stand mixer and a dough hook it is a lot easier. Cover again and leave in a warm place to rise until doubled in size (about 1 hour).

Knock back the dough and gently knead in the raisins. Divide into 6 pieces (each about 65g/2¼oz) and form these into tight balls. Transfer to a lined baking sheet (spaced well apart, about 2cm/¾in). Cover with oiled cling film and leave until at least doubled in size (about 1 hour, but don't worry if it takes longer, you need to make sure they're definitely doubled in size). At this time, preheat the oven to 200°C fan (220°C/425°F/gas mark 7).

Bake for 10 minutes until golden brown. Remove from the oven, transfer to a wire rack to cool.

Once the buns are cool, beat all the icing ingredients together, leave to rest for 1 minute and then pour over the buns. These are best eaten the same day.

Here is another Easter bread, that harks from Bulgaria, that it would be a shame to only eat at one time in the year. It is essentially a plaited enriched loaf, similar to the Jewish challah or the Swiss zopf. The honey and the egg wash ensure you get a lacquered finish that should be a deep golden brown. The crumb of this bread is all about the fragrance, a fusion of the saffron, honey, citrus, vanilla and, of course, that winey yeastiness. When referring to saffron, you might wonder what is a pinch? I love saffron, so go for a fat-fingered pinch and don't mind if the flavour dominates, or you can go more subtle and well balanced if you please. In Bulgaria the flavourings in this loaf vary, but plump raisins and the plaited shape is a must.

Pinch of saffron threads

200ml (7fl oz) warm water

50g (2oz) raisins

450g (1lb) strong white bread flour

50g (2oz) strong wholemeal (whole-wheat) bread flour

10g (¼oz) instant yeast

Heaped ½ tsp salt

100ml (3½fl oz) semi-skimmed milk

40g (1½oz) unsalted softened butter (at room temperature)

30g (1oz) runny honey

1 tsp vanilla paste

Zest of 1 lemon, or 10 drops lemon oil

25g (1oz) grated butternut squash or carrot

1 egg

10g (¼oz) pearl sugar nibs

10g (¼oz) caster (superfine) sugar

Kozunak plait

Soak the saffron in a bowl with the warm water for 10 minutes. Add the raisins to a heatproof bowl, just cover with boiling water and also leave to soak for 10 minutes.

Toss the flours, yeast and salt together, then add the milk and saffron water and mix to form a shaggy dough (until the dough has just come together, it doesn't need to be smooth at this stage). Cover with beeswax wrap or clingfilm and leave to rest for 15 minutes.

Knead for 1 minute in the bowl, then add the butter, honey, vanilla, lemon zest or oil and grated butternut squash or carrot, and continue to knead until incorporated (it will be very sticky at first – you can use a dough hook in a stand mixer). Drain the raisins and gently knead into the dough. Cover and leave in a warm place until doubled in size (about 1 hour).

Knock back the dough, then decide how you want to plait the bread. I like going for a traditional three-strand plait, but you can find all kinds of fancy ways to do this on YouTube.

Place on a lined baking tray, cover with an oiled piece of cling film and leave to rise until doubled in size (about 30 minutes, but don't worry if it t akes longer). Preheat the oven to 200°C fan (220°C/425°F/gas mark 7).

Beat the egg and egg wash the plait with a soft brush, sprinkle with the sugar nibs, then the sugar and bake for 5 minutes, then reduce the oven temperature to 180°C fan (200°C/400°F/gas mark 6) and bake for a further 25 minutes. Leave to cool slightly before tearing and sharing.

Best eaten fresh, but will last for up to 3 days and is great toasted.

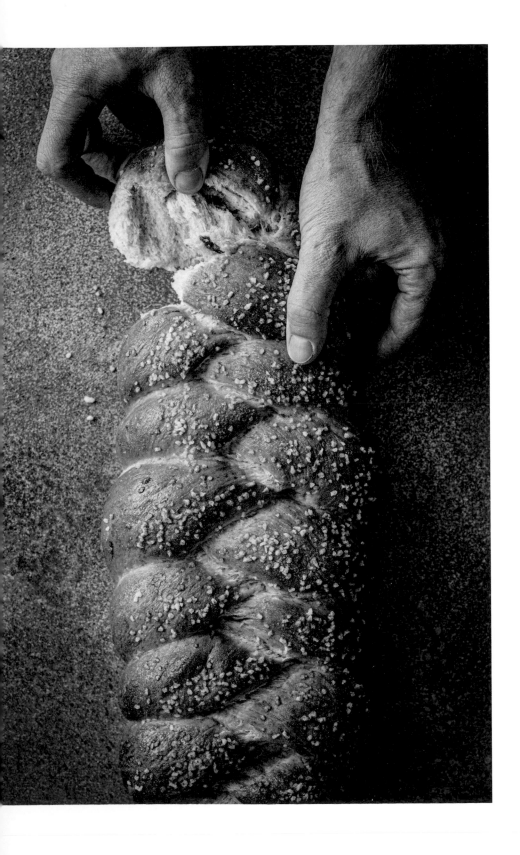

Treats that travel

*home-made snacks too
good to leave behind*

Is there anything better than going on a long hike or bike ride, then stopping for a breather and pulling a tasty, home-made treat out of your bag? You sit there, on a park bench or next to a river, eating your sticky, sweet or chewy treat, then lick your fingers afterwards to eke out every last little scrap of flavour. Frankly, sometimes it's the best part of the whole outing! Afterwards, you feel renewed, ready to tackle the journey home.

Even if you think of yourself as someone who doesn't snack, the truth is we all get peckish when we're out and about, especially if you've been working up a sweat. Would you rather have a slice of Sticky malt loaf (see page 212) or a home-made energy ball (see page 208) on hand, or run into the nearest newsagents and grab a bag of crisps or an ultra-processed snack bar? Me, I like to be prepared and have something stashed about my person. You know, just in case. (Who am I kidding? As if I could have a thick slice of malt loaf in my bag and not eat it.)

This chapter contains treats that are perfect for taking with you on the road. And if you're not off on a big hike or cycle ride, why not make a batch of something to take into work to treat your colleagues? Whip out a Tupperware of Fig rolls (see page 198), for instance, and you'll be everyone's new best friend (as long as they like figs!). They're one of my all-time favourite things to bake (and eat), and I was thrilled when we had fig rolls as a technical challenge on *Bake Off*. You could say I had something of an advantage that week.

These recipes store really well, so you can make a batch and keep it for days, and they travel well, meaning they won't dry out if they spend the day wrapped in paper or packaged up in a box. (Which also makes them great to keep on hand at home as a post-work snack.) All are designed to give you energy and fuel to tide you over to the next mealtime, without scrimping on that all-important rich, sweet hit. And they're ideal for sharing with others – which is, after all, part of the joy of baking.

*Peanut butter is my favourite food and it marries so well with the form of a cookie.
Its gloopy thick texture provides a very good base, and is a healthier alternative to a
traditional cookie fat. The nuts, wholemeal flour, oats and seeds in this mix give a good
microbiome feed, and you can up the nutritional content further by adding 20g (¾oz)
of other seeds to the mix. Vanilla, toasted sesame oil, malt extract and cinnamon all
harmonise with peanut flavour, but give the cookie a more complex flavour infusion.*

150g (5oz) peanut butter

50g (2oz) unsalted butter

20ml (¾fl oz) toasted
    sesame oil

150g (5oz) soft brown sugar

1 medium egg

1 tsp vanilla extract

1 tsp malt extract

½ tsp ground cinnamon

75g (3oz) plain
    (all-purpose) flour

75g (3oz) wholemeal plain
    (whole-wheat
    all-purpose) flour

½ tsp bicarbonate of soda
    (baking soda)

40g (1½oz) rolled oats

10g (¼oz) ground flaxseeds

Sesame seeds for sprinkling
    (approx. 10g/¼oz)

Rock salt, for sprinkling

Peanut sesame cookies

Preheat the oven to 180°C fan (200°C/400°F/gas mark 6), and
prepare two baking trays with baking parchment.

Beat together the peanut butter, butter, sesame oil, sugar, egg, vanilla,
malt extract and cinnamon until smooth.

Put the flours, bicarbonate of soda (baking soda), oats and flaxseeds
into a mixing bowl and toss together.

Combine the wet and dry ingredients to form a smooth dough. Sprinkle
the sesame seeds onto a plate.

With a teaspoon scoop up 30g (1oz) portions, dip into the sesame seeds
(you're not looking for a full coverage, just the effect of a sprinkling),
place on the tray, and press down so that they form at least 2cm discs.

Bake for 15 minutes, then allow to cool for 5 minutes before transferring
to a wire rack to cool fully.

Fig rolls are one of my absolute faves. I can't understand what there isn't to like – a soft, crumbly, fragrant pastry enveloping a sticky mass of rich dried fruit. They also travel well and don't go stale quickly, so they are brilliant for a cycling holiday or a hike. Although a treat, they are packed with goodness from the prunes, figs and almonds. If I can't persuade you that they are the king of treats, can I at least persuade you to give them a go? The pastry is somewhat tricky to use as it is quite crumbly, but you needn't worry if it falls apart slightly as you can push it all together.

100g (3½oz) unsalted butter

2 tsp vanilla extract

70g (2½oz) semolina, plus extra for rolling

160g (5½oz) plain (all-purpose) flour, plus extra for dusting

30g (1oz) wholemeal plain (whole-wheat all-purpose) flour

½ tsp baking powder

¼ tsp salt

50g (2oz) ground almonds

100g (3½oz) caster (superfine) sugar

1 large egg

Filling:

250g (9oz) soft dried figs

200g (7oz) prunes

Classic fig rolls

Gently melt the butter in a small saucepan with the vanilla extract on a low heat. Put the semolina, flours, baking powder, salt, ground almonds and sugar into a bowl and pour over the melted butter. Mix together, then add the egg and bring together to make a dough. Wrap in a beeswax cloth (or cling film) and put in the fridge for 1 hour.

In a food processor, blitz the figs and prunes to a paste, then transfer to a bowl, cover and put in the fridge along with the pastry.

Remove the pastry from the fridge and gently knead it on a lightly floured surface until pliable, then roll it out to 30cm x 20cm (12in x 8in) rectangle. The pastry is very crumbly, so be patient and gentle (don't worry too much as you can fix cracks later). Cut down the middle so that you have two rectangles each 10cm x 30cm (4in x 12in). Take half the filling and put this into the centre of the rectangle, fold the pastry over and seal with a little water. If the roll is very cracked, apply some water with your fingers and then spread down the pastry with the back of a knife until smooth. Do the same with the next rectangle.

Sprinkle semolina over the work surface and gently roll the pastry around in this. Take a really sharp knife and cut it into 20 pieces altogether. Place on a lined baking tray and chill for 15 minutes.

Preheat the oven to 190°C fan (210°C/400°F/gas mark 6) and when the rolls are chilled, bake for 15 minutes until nicely golden at the edges.

Once baked, cool on a wire rack. These can be stored in an airtight container for up to a week, but they are best eaten within the first 3 days.

Apparently, Yorkshire parkin is traditionally eaten on Bonfire Night, but our family had toffee apples on 5 November and parkin was a year-round staple. How have ginger cakes become synonymous with stodge, denseness and stickiness? I'm not sure of the history but I love it. A good ginger parkin should be sweet and sticky, so that you can up the ginger spice without it getting bitter. My mum's parkin has oats and wholemeal (whole-wheat) flour, and I've made it my own with the addition of quinoa, sweet potato and prunes to up the nutritional content. I've gone a bit rogue here by using a round tin and then cutting it into squares. I like disordered order sometimes, and the choice of different-sized pieces at the edges. If this offends your sense of balance, you can bake it in the same way in a 20cm (8in) square tin.

serves 12

100g (3½oz) butter
100g (3½oz) soft brown sugar
100g (3½oz) golden syrup
50g (2oz) malt extract
30g (1oz) prunes
100g (3½oz) cooked quinoa
1 large egg
120g (4½oz) plain
(all-purpose) flour
50g (2oz) wholemeal plain
(whole-wheat
all-purpose) flour
2 tsp baking powder
170g (6oz) porridge oats
(oatmeal)
2 tsp ground ginger
(or 3 tsp if you're brave)
60g (2¼oz) finely grated
sweet potato

Mum's Yorkshire parkin

Preheat the oven to 180°C fan (200°C/400°F/gas mark 6). Line a 23cm (9in) round springform cake tin with baking parchment.

Add the butter, sugar, syrup, malt extract and prunes to a small saucepan and cook on a medium heat to gently melt the butter and dissolve the sugar. Allow to cool for 10 minutes, then transfer to a blender and blend with the quinoa for 1 minute. Add the egg and continue blending for 10 seconds.

In a large mixing bowl, add the flours, baking powder, oats and ginger, and toss together.

Pour the batter from the blender over the dry ingredients and mix to combine. Add the sweet potato and continue to stir until fully mixed. Transfer to the tin and bake for 35 minutes or until a skewer inserted in the middle of the cake comes out clean.

Once baked, allow to cool on a wire rack, and for best results pack into an airtight container and leave for a day before cutting into squares and eating. This will last for 1 week, but is better eaten in the first 3 days.

Treats that travel

I'm from Yorkshire so I know a good fat rascal. It is basically an enriched scone that can be eaten without jam or cream. I love taking these out on a hike or as a pick-me-up for work in the afternoon. You can play around with the flavours all you like; they can take robust and heavy spicing, soft and light fragrance, a substantial tangy zing or simply vanilla. Below is my favourite combination, but coming close in at number two is adding chunks of Bramley or Braeburn apples and rose water.

150g (5oz) unsalted butter

250g (9oz) plain (all-purpose) flour, plus extra for dusting

50g (2oz) wholemeal (whole-wheat) spelt flour

1 tsp baking powder

½ tsp bicarbonate of soda (baking soda)

70g (2½oz) caster (superfine) sugar, plus extra to sprinkle

Zest of 1 orange (or 10 drops of orange oil)

½ tsp ground cinnamon

½ tsp allspice

¼ tsp grated nutmeg

150g (5oz) dark chocolate (70% cocoa solids), coarsely chopped

50g (2oz) currants

50g (2oz) raisins

2 eggs

75ml (3fl oz) semi-skimmed milk

10ml (¼fl oz) lemon juice

100g (3½oz) chopped hazelnuts

Spicy fat rascals

Preheat the oven to 180°C fan (200°C/400°F/gas mark 6). Line a baking tray with baking parchment.

In a large mixing bowl, rub the butter with the flours, baking powder and bicarbonate of soda (baking soda) until it resembles breadcrumbs (you can do this in a stand mixer using the beater paddle, if you prefer).

Add the sugar, orange zest or oil, spices, chocolate and dried fruit and mix together. Whisk 1 egg with the milk and lemon juice, then add to the dry mix. Work gently to form a dough (do not over-knead). The dough will be quite sticky.

Divide the dough into 8 pieces, about 100g (3½oz) each, and roll them into balls. You can use a dusting of flour to help if it is very sticky. Put the chopped hazelnuts into a bowl, whisk the other egg, then dip each ball into the egg wash, then the hazelnuts, then place on the lined baking tray nut-side up. Sprinkle with a little extra sugar.

Bake for 18 minutes then transfer to a wire rack to cool. These store well in an airtight container for 3–5 days.

A sweet biscuit is the perfect accompaniment to bitter coffee, and if you're going to choose one, nibbling soft Italian amaretti biscuits between sips would be hard to beat. In this recipe the grated carrot keeps them soft and adds natural sweetness, and the cooked rice gives a more substantial chew without detracting from the crumbly delicacy of a biscuit made predominantly with ground almonds.

Amaretti biscuits generally use egg white to bind and give a chewy texture. I wanted to make a vegan version so have replaced the egg white with aquafaba (the liquid from a can of chickpeas/garbanzo beans). I don't know who decided to try whipping chickpea water, but they found an egg-cellent vegan egg white replacement that is perfect for meringues, macarons, mousse and . . . amaretti.

75g (3oz) aquafaba

1 small carrot (about 70g/2½oz), finely grated

1 tsp almond extract

100g (3½oz) cooked white rice

125g (4½oz) caster (superfine) sugar

200g (7oz) ground almonds

40g (1½oz) plain (all-purpose) flour (gluten-free works well)

Granulated sugar, for coating

Aquafaba soft amaretti

Preheat the oven to 150°C fan (170°C/325°F/gas mark 3).

In a clean bowl, whisk the aquafaba to stiff peaks. In a separate bowl, mix the carrot with the almond extract. Put the cooked rice and sugar in a beaker and blend with a hand blender.

In a mixing bowl, combine the ground almonds and flour then fold in a tablespoon of the aquafaba followed by the carrot mix, then the rice and sugar mix. Fold in the rest of the aquafaba in two stages.

Make 25g (1oz) balls of mix, roll them in the granulated sugar, and place on a lined baking sheet (2cm/¾in apart). Bake for 25 minutes, then allow to cool fully before eating.

From left to right: Sticky malt loaf (see page 212), Aquafaba soft ameretti (see page 205), Spicy fat rascals (see page 202).

Raw food energy snacks are all the rage right now. They are so expensive to buy, but so easy and cheap to make. My version gives you quick-release sugars from the fruit, slow-release energy from the oats, theobromine from the chocolate and a whole lot of flavour to give you that delicious but nutritious treat while you are exercising. Theobromine is a caffeine-like compound in chocolate that really gives an energy boost, plus the melted chocolate emulsifies the other ingredients to give a smooth and workable mixture.

60g (2oz) porridge oats (oatmeal)

50g (2oz) dark chocolate, melted (I use 70% cocoa solids, but you can go as low as 40%)

70g (2½oz) dates

70g (2½oz) prunes

10 drops of orange oil or zest of 1 orange

1 tbsp cocoa powder

30g (1oz) cocoa nibs

Dark choc energy balls

Blitz the oats in a food processor until broken up, but not a powder.

Melt the chocolate in a bain-marie or a bowl set over a pan of simmering water, but make sure the base of the bowl is not touching the water.

Blitz the dates, prunes, orange oil and cocoa powder to a paste in a food processor, then continue to blitz while adding the melted chocolate. Scoop the mixture into a mixing bowl.

Knead in the oats and cocoa nibs, then take handfuls of the mixture and roll into 30g (1oz) balls.

The balls last for 5–7 days in an airtight container stored in a cool cupboard, or the fridge.

A good scone is fluffy and light, barely sweet and calling out for a good jam. A scone has a markedly lower fat and sugar content to a regular cake, making them a much healthier sweet treat. The trick to a great scone is not to overwork the mix. While rubbing the butter into the flour you don't want the butter to melt, so cold hands work best. I have very warm hands so I often start by mashing it with a fork, or you can throw it into the stand mixer for 3 minutes using the beater paddle. You do not want to knead this dough, it should just be brought together so that you're not developing the gluten.

This recipe works very well with vegan spreads and non-dairy milk, and I like to serve them topped with jam, Greek yogurt, fruit and a dusting of icing (confectioners') sugar.

80g (3oz) unsalted butter

300g (10oz) plain (all-purpose) flour, plus extra for dusting

50g (2oz) wholemeal plain (whole-wheat all-purpose) flour

1 tsp baking powder

½ tsp bicarbonate of soda (baking soda)

Pinch of salt

50g (2oz) caster (superfine) sugar

1 tsp lemon juice

170ml (6fl oz) semi-skimmed milk

Straight-up scones

Preheat the oven to 180°C fan (200°C/400°F/gas mark 6) with a baking tray inside.

Rub the butter into the flours, baking powder, bicarbonate of soda (baking soda), salt and sugar until they resemble breadcrumbs.

Add the lemon juice to the milk, then pour this over the dry ingredients. Gently mix to combine into a soft dough (do not knead, this will make the scones tough).

Leave to sit for 5 minutes, then turn out onto a lightly floured surface and roll to a 2cm (¾in) thickness. Cut out the scones using a 4cm (1½in) biscuit cutter. Push the excess back together to form a dough (again, do not knead), then roll out again to 2cm (¾in) and continue until you've used all the mix.

Take the baking tray out of the oven, line with baking parchment, add the scones and bake for 10–12 minutes until golden. Leave to cool on a wire rack.

Malt extract

There's an old 1980s American advert where a kid drinks
his Ovaltine then can't stop leaping around in delight.
'I can't get over Ovaltine,' goes the annoyingly cheery jingle.
I never got over the rich malty taste of Ovaltine either.
In a good way, of course.

If, like me, you love the flavour of Maltesers, malt loaf
and, yes, a cheeky mug of Ovaltine, get yourself a jar of
malt extract. You'll love the mellow background note it
brings to bakes.

A super-short history of malt extract

We bakers owe a lot to the brewing industry. As well as giving us baker's yeast – which transformed breadmaking and is still the most common way of making bread today – brewing gave us malt extract.

Malt is made by soaking barley grains to germinate them, then drying the grains with hot air (a process known as 'malting'). This process quickly turns the starches in the grain into sugars, which are extracted by mashing the grains. The resulting sugary liquid is concentrated down to produce the sweet, treacly substance we know as malt extract.

The use of malt extract in brewing really took off in the 1800s, when a technique was invented to speed up the concentration process. During America's Prohibition era, brewers began selling malt extract to survive, often marketing the malt extract as 'hop-flavoured'. Which makes you wonder just how many people were buying it for home brews!

Malt extract also has a long history as a health product. By the early 1900s, malt extract was being used as a nutritional enhancer for working-class British children. Before that, Captain Cook – who sailed his ships from my hometown, Whitby – gave his sailors malt extract to prevent scurvy. Although lemons were found to be just as effective, and cheaper . . .

How to use this hero ingredient

These days, you'll find malt extract for sale in many supermarkets and health food shops, as well as online. You'll be amazed how useful it is. And not just in malt loaf. Malt extract is brilliant for breadmaking, giving extra flavour and a deep mahogany crust to breads and bagels. It's also great paired with vanilla in sweet bakes, as it deepens the vanilla flavour and adds a muggy richness.

I sometimes use diastatic malt powder in my home baking, particularly in breads. For the recipes in this book, I've specified regular old malt extract, but I'd definitely advise giving the malt powder a try in your breads. Add a teaspoon to your dough and see what happens.

You'll find malt extract in my:

- Simnel cake bites (see page 182)
- Vegan coffee layer cake (see page 186)
- Mum's Yorkshire parkin (see page 201)
- Sticky malt loaf (see page 212)
- Morning baked bagels (see page 60)

Malt loaf is well-known in the cycling community as a perfect high-carb, low-fat snack. The sugar and dried fruit gives you a speedy dose of energy, but it also contains slow-release carbohydrates that are perfect for endurance. This malt loaf also happens to be a delicious treat in its own right. Its chewy-yet-soft texture means it's easy to eat when you're in the saddle, but it also works just as well back at home — toasted, buttered and partnered with a cup of tea.

50g (2oz) prunes

50g (2oz) dried figs

50g (2oz) raisins

150g (5oz) malt extract, plus extra for brushing

2 tsp instant coffee granules

50g (2oz) soft brown sugar

50g (2oz) dark muscovado (brown) sugar

50g (2oz) cooked white rice

60g (2oz) strong white bread flour

150g (5oz) plain (all-purpose) flour

¼ tsp salt

1½ tsp baking powder

2 large eggs

Sticky malt loaf

Preheat the oven to 160°C fan (180°C/350°F/gas mark 4). Line a 20cm (8in) loaf tin with baking parchment.

Chop the prunes and dried figs into pieces the same size as your raisins and set all the dried fruit aside.

In a saucepan, gently heat the malt extract, coffee granules, 110ml (3½fl oz) water and the sugars until dissolved. Pour this into a beaker with the cooked rice and blend with a hand blender until smooth.

In a mixing bowl, combine the flours, salt and baking powder. Pour over the sugar mixture and combine before beating in the eggs. Finally, stir through the dried fruit to evenly distribute.

Transfer to the lined loaf tin and bake for 1 hour or until a skewer inserted in the middle of the cake comes out clean.

Allow to cool for 10 minutes before turning out onto a wire rack, then brush with malt extract. This is a sticky loaf, so my tip is to slice it with a sharp bread knife once cool.

I store mine wrapped in baking parchment. It will last for up to 7 days, but after day 4 is best toasted.

If you are looking for a quick, no-faff, healthy baked treat, these could be your answer. They have a rich chocolateyness, but the banana flavour reveals its healthy credentials. The building blocks for these cakes are not just butter and sugar, but banana, sweet potato, yogurt, olive oil and cooked quinoa. The cooked quinoa and the grated sweet potato provide substance, moistness and sweetness, which are essential for a good muffin but are also so good for you. The quinoa provides protein and essential amino acids, the sweet potato provides vitamin A and they both deliver a good portion of fibre. A great treat for you, your kids, friends and family (unless they don't like chocolate . . . or bananas).

Banana chocolate muffins

100g (3½oz) dark chocolate (70% cocoa solids), chopped into chunks

130g (4½oz) plain (all-purpose) flour

30g (1oz) cocoa powder

100g (3½oz) soft brown sugar

2 tsp baking powder

1 very ripe banana, chopped

30g (1oz) natural yogurt

50ml (2fl oz) light olive oil

1 large egg

1 tsp vanilla extract

100g (3½oz) cooked quinoa

50g (2oz) finely grated sweet potato

Runny honey, to glaze (optional)

Preheat the oven to 200°C fan (220°C/425°F/gas mark 7). Prepare a muffin tray either by greasing or filling 10 holes with paper cases.

Add the chocolate to a mixing bowl with the flour, cocoa, sugar, baking powder, and toss together. Blend the banana, yogurt, oil, egg, vanilla and quinoa until smooth, then add to a bowl with the sweet potato. Combine the wet and dry ingredients with a wooden spoon until just mixed, then divide between the paper cases or muffin tin holes.

Bake for 5 minutes, then reduce the oven temperature to 150°C fan (170°C/325°F/gas mark 3) and bake for a further 12–15 minutes, or until a toothpick inserted in the centre comes out clean. If you like, glaze the tops with honey while they're still a little warm. Best eaten fresh but stored in an airtight container will last for up to 5 days.

Perfect puds

*happy endings for
any day of the week*

Who doesn't love eating a proper pudding? And by proper pudding, I mean a home-made dessert. The full stop that comes after a nice meal. Something that's usually (but not always) served warm from the oven. The sort of thing you eat with a spoon, scraping the last of the gooey sweetness off the sides of the bowl or glass at the end.

I might be wrong, but I get the sense that desserts aren't as popular among bakers as they used to be, having been ousted by cakes and other sweet treats. And while I could happily eat a slice of cake or some fig rolls after dinner, nothing quite hits the post-meal spot like a good pud. Dessert is just more… deliberate.

Plus there's something comforting and old-school about puddings. Growing up in the Atherton house, my favourite school-night dessert was yogurt and mashed banana, topped with crumbs from the flapjack tin. On a weekend it was always crumble. The way I remember it, we had a crumble every weekend (we had a lot of fruit trees in the garden), but it probably wasn't quite that often. These days, I still enjoy a good pudding, but I usually only make one at the weekend or when we have people round for dinner — when I have more time to get something in the oven. (I'm not sure how people would react if I served them mashed banana and yogurt for dessert!)

You'll no doubt recognise the classic puddings in this chapter, but I've given some of them a new twist, adding the sorts of flavours I like to eat, such as fennel (which gives a gentle sweet anise flavour to the tuile wafers that accompany my Kombucha granita – see page 225). Then there's my Aperol crumble pots (see page 228), perfect for Aperol spritz lovers. But, underneath it all, these are still the same types of puddings that have been gracing our tables for generations. So if you're out of the habit of making and eating a proper home-made dessert, these recipes will get you back into the swing of it.

It's true that puddings can be a fairly indulgent (some would say heavy) way to end a meal. Whenever I'm making one, I like to serve a lighter dinner beforehand so that the pudding is the star of the show. But there aren't any rules. These work brilliantly after any kind of meal, on any day of the week, even at any time of the day. In fact, I often have leftover crumble for breakfast, and in the summer, sometimes I skip dinner and go straight to dessert.

The bold and bright plum is the star of this pudding, but it is lifted by a subtle flavour profile including grapefruit, sweet almond, Thai basil, cinnamon and honey. Upside-down cakes are pretty substantial sponge cakes, but the body of this pudding is more similar to a frangipane, which is a velvety almond pudding usually encased in pastry. I love making this dessert in the late summer when the plums are deliciously sweet and you can fit in a substantial dessert following a salad. This recipe is perfect if you need to avoid gluten.

Plum upside-down frangipane

8 plums, stoned and cut into 5mm (¼in) slices

Zest and juice of 1 pink grapefruit

90g (3¼oz) unsalted butter, plus 15g (½oz) for greasing

150g (5oz) caster (superfine) sugar

4 large eggs

200g (7oz) ground almonds

60g (2oz) gluten-free flour

1 tsp baking powder

50g (2oz) finely grated butternut squash

10g (¼oz) soft brown sugar

Cinnamon yogurt:

300g (10½oz) Greek yogurt

1 tsp ground cinnamon

10ml (¼fl oz) runny honey

Glaze:

25g (1oz) caster (superfine) sugar

2 sprigs of Thai basil, leaves torn

Put the plums into a medium saucepan with the juice of the grapefruit and simmer for 5 minutes with a lid on (or until the plums are starting to get soft, but still very much hold their shape). Remove the plums and set aside, keeping the juice in the pan.

Preheat the oven to 170°C fan (190°C/375°F/gas mark 5).

In a mixing bowl, cream the 90g (3¼oz) butter and the caster (superfine) sugar together, then add the eggs one at a time (don't worry, it will look a little curdled). Next, stir through the ground almonds, flour, grapefruit zest, baking powder and butternut squash.

Grease a Bundt tin, about 20cm (8in) – you can use a spray. Melt the 15g (½oz) butter and pour this evenly over the bottom of the tin, then sprinkle with the brown sugar. Arrange the plums across the bottom (make sure they are tightly packed as they will shrink slightly when cooked). Pour over the batter and bake for 40 minutes or until a skewer inserted into the centre comes out clean.

While the pudding is baking, make the cinnamon yogurt. Mix the yogurt, cinnamon and honey together until smooth.

Once the pudding is baked, leave for 5 minutes, then turn upside down on a plate.

To make the glaze, add the sugar to the pan with the reserved juices (from the plums) along with the torn Thai basil leaves, and reduce on a medium heat until it forms a syrup. Pour this over the pudding through a sieve and it is ready to serve. Best eaten fresh but any leftovers stored in an airtight container will last for up to 5 days.

This dessert resembles a baked cheesecake, but its moussey, light filling is made from a can of peaches and ground almonds with no cream cheese or cream in sight. It is so light that it sinks in the middle when baking, but don't worry, it is meant to be like this, and this is the perfect cavity for the yogurt and fruit topping. The crumble base has a gentle spice, but if you want to take it up a few notches, peaches match well with most warm spices, so you can try adding nutmeg, cardamom, star anise, fennel or pepper too. This dessert is perfect for a cooler summer evening.

Peaches on ginger dessert

Crust:

70g (2½oz) plain (all-purpose) flour

30g (1oz) wholemeal plain (whole-wheat all-purpose) flour

1 tsp ground cinnamon

½ tsp ground ginger

½ tsp baking powder

40g (1½oz) soft brown sugar

75g (3oz) unsalted butter

Filling:

4 large eggs

80g (3oz) caster (superfine) sugar

1 x 375g (15oz) can peaches in juice (drained weight 330g/11½oz)

60g (2oz) runny honey

170g (6oz) ground almonds

1 tsp baking powder

Topping:

150g (5oz) Greek yogurt

Zest and juice of 1 lemon

20g (¾oz) flaked (slivered) almonds, plus extra for sprinkling

200g (7oz) honey

4 cloves

2 ripe peaches, stoned and thinly sliced

Preheat the oven to 150°C fan (170°C/325°F/gas mark 3). Prepare a 20cm (8in) springform tin with baking parchment.

Rub the flours, cinnamon, ginger, baking powder and sugar with the butter until it forms breadcrumbs. Press into the base of the tin and bake for 20 minutes, then leave to cool in the tin.

Turn the oven temperature up to 170°C fan (190°C/375°F/gas mark 5).

Whisk the eggs and the sugar together in a mixing bowl until light and creamy and doubled in volume.

In a blender whizz the canned peaches with the honey until smooth. In a mixing bowl, mix the ground almonds and baking powder with the peach mixture. Pour in half the egg mixture and fold, followed by the second half, then fold until just incorporated. Pour over the biscuit base and smooth the top.

Bake for 25 minutes, then add a foil sheet or baking parchment on top of the tin, and bake for a further 15 minutes.

While it bakes, make the topping. Mix the yogurt together with the lemon zest and juice. Gently toast the almonds in a dry frying pan on a medium heat. As soon as they start to brown, tip them onto a plate. Put the honey in a small saucepan with the cloves and simmer for about 8 minutes until the honey turns a deep golden amber. Remove the cloves.

Slice the ginger dessert and serve with a dollop of the yogurt, some peach slices, a drizzle of the burnt honey and a sprinkling of the almonds.

I love picking blackberries each autumn (although now in the UK it is more like summer). I get a bit obsessed and often have a competition with my twin brother about who can forage the most each season. My freezer gets full for the rest of the year, but if you don't want scratched and nettle-stung knees, you can substitute shop-bought frozen raspberries. Growing up we had an apple orchard. This makes it sound very grand, please don't think neat rows of trees in a rolling orchard, instead picture eight higgledy-piggledy trees at the bottom of the garden – four Bramley and four Cox. I loved climbing the trees to pick the apples, and I loved our weekly crumbles that we made with them. Crumble topping is sweet and buttery so you don't need to make your fruit sticky and caramelised, a thick layer of soft unsweetened fruit is the dream. Traditionally crumble topping is made with butter, sugar and flour, but I've added oats and almonds to provide a different texture, flavour and to amp up the nutritional value.

serves 8

500g (1lb 2oz) cooking (I use Bramley or Braeburn) apples, peeled, cored and chopped into chunks

200g (7oz) blackberries (or frozen raspberries)

40g (1½oz) unsalted butter

1 tsp almond extract

40g (1½oz) plain (all-purpose) flour

40g (1½oz) soft brown sugar

20g (¾oz) ground almonds

40g (1½oz) porridge oats (oatmeal)

30g (1oz) flaked (slivered) almonds

Apple and blackberry almond crumble

I use a 20cm (8in) loaf tin for this recipe as I don't have lots of fancy dishes, but it would look great in a medium ceramic casserole dish.

Add the apples to a medium saucepan filled with cold water, then drain the water away (the residual water coating the apples is enough to cook them). Put a lid on the saucepan, place it on a low heat and cook for 5 minutes, shaking the pan every minute to rotate the apples. The apples will cook some more when baked with the crumble, but you decide if you want them to have a little bite, or cook them for another 5 minutes if you like the apples softer.

Once cooked, remove the lid, add the blackberries and stir through. Spoon into the dish and set aside.

Preheat the oven to 200°C fan (220°C/425°F/gas mark 7).

Rub the butter, almond extract and flour together in a bowl with your fingertips to create crumbs. Add the sugar and ground almonds and continue rubbing together. Stir through the oats and flaked (slivered) almonds and sprinkle the crumble mix over the fruit.

Bake for 20 minutes or until you are happy with the crumble colour. Allow to cool before eating.

This dessert is guaranteed to impress but it is also light, so perfect to follow a heavy main meal, or to finish a summer evening. Tuiles are a crisp thin wafer and sound faffy to make, but they are not difficult, and when you get them right you'll feel very accomplished. Choose an unpasteurised kombucha, as this ensures all the beneficial bacteria are present. If you're going with a plain kombucha, I've suggested adding some ginger.

Granita:

500ml (16fl oz) kombucha

50g (2oz) honey

1 tsp minced fresh root
  ginger (optional)

Tuile:

20g (¾oz) unsalted pistachios

35g (1¼oz) unsalted butter,
  softened

30g (1oz) icing
  (confectioners') sugar

1 large egg white

35g (1¼oz) plain
  (all-purpose) flour

1 tsp fennel seeds

Flaky sea salt

Natural live yogurt, to serve

Kombucha granita and fennel tuile

Mix together the kombucha, honey and ginger, if using, then pour into a deep baking tray and place in the freezer for 4 hours. Set a timer every 45 minutes, then remove the tray and fork through to break it into crystals before returning it to the freezer.

To make the tuile, prepare the pistachios by either crushing them in a pestle and mortar or giving them a quick pulse in a food processor, then set aside. Preheat the oven to 180°C fan (200°C/400°F/gas mark 6).

Beat the butter and icing sugar together until smooth. Add the egg white and beat until combined and smooth. Leave to rest for 15 minutes.

Take a teaspoon of the mix and drop it onto a baking tray lined with baking parchment or a silicone mat (my favourite here, as they are really non-stick and ideal to help you move fast when they come out of the oven). Spread it out to about 5cm (2in) diameter (as thin as you can) and sprinkle with the pulsed nuts, fennel seeds and salt. Continue until you have covered your tray, leaving 1cm (½in) between each biscuit. You could spread the mixture across a stencil to get a perfect edge and shape.

Bake for 5–7 minutes until golden at the edges – the timing will depend a lot on your oven, you don't want them to be white as they will end up chewy. If you want to set your tuile into shapes, work very quickly once they are out of the oven – lift them with a palette knife onto a mould like a rolling pin. The biscuits will set hard very quickly as they cool; if they've hardened too quickly you can place them back in the oven for 20 seconds to soften again. I like to use a baguette baking tray, as I don't make a lot of baguettes so it's nice to have another use for it.

To serve, scrape the granita with a spoon and place in a glass with a dollop of yogurt and a couple of tuile.

*Left: Peaches on ginger
dessert (see page 221).
Right: Boozy Bakewell
tart (see page 231).*

Okay, so crumbles are my favourite dessert, as you can see because here's another variation on the theme. This crumble is more stylish, the kind I'd serve if I have guests (this is as stylish as I get). Aperol is a really interesting aperitif from Italy which includes flavours of rhubarb and bitter orange. Why not bookend a summer dinner party with an Aperol spritz as an aperitif and these Aperol crumble pots as the dessert? The crumble topping is sweet and crunchy but packed full of all the good stuff from the granola (see page 44) – seeds, nuts, whole grains. It is a treat of a dessert, but with clandestine nutritional benefits.

300g (10oz) rhubarb, cut into 2cm (¾in) chunks

50ml (2fl oz) Aperol

20g (¾oz) caster (superfine) sugar

Greek yogurt, to serve

Crumble topping:

25g (1oz) unsalted butter

10 drops of orange oil (or the zest of 1 orange)

10ml (¼fl oz) toasted sesame oil

30g (1oz) plain (all-purpose) flour

30g (1oz) wholemeal plain (whole-wheat all-purpose) flour

½ tsp baking powder

25g (1oz) soft brown sugar

100g (3½oz) THIS is granola (page 44) or shop-bought granola

Aperol crumble pots

Place the rhubarb chunks in a saucepan with 1 tablespoon of water. Put a lid on, place the pan on a low heat and cook for 10 minutes, shaking the pan every minute to rotate the fruit. The rhubarb should be just starting to go soft, but still holding its shape. Remove the fruit with a slotted spoon and divide between 4 individual ramekins.

Add the Aperol to the juices left in the pan from cooking the fruit, along with the sugar and gently heat to a simmer. Continue simmering until it has reduced to a syrup, then pour this over the fruit in the pie dishes.

Preheat the oven to 200°C fan (220°C/425°F/gas mark 7).

Rub the butter, orange oil, sesame oil, flours, baking powder and sugar together until they resemble breadcrumbs. Stir through the granola and sprinkle over each fruit base in the pots.

Transfer the ramekins to a baking tray and bake for 15 minutes or until you are happy with the crumble colour. Allow to cool for 10 minutes before serving with a dollop of Greek yogurt.

A Bakewell tart is a great way to practise your shortcrust pastry-making skills because the frangipane filling is not too wet and therefore you don't need to worry about a soggy bottom. This is a Bakewell with a difference; it has wholemeal flour, seeds, dried fruit and sweet potato. I've used rum as I think it marries particularly well with prunes, but if you have another liquor in your cupboard that needs using up feel free to substitute it.

Boozy Bakewell tart

Pastry:

130g (4½oz) plain (all-purpose) flour, plus extra for dusting

70g (2½oz) wholemeal plain (whole-wheat all-purpose) flour

40g (1½oz) icing (confectioners') sugar

Pinch of salt

100g (3½oz) unsalted butter

1 egg

10ml (¼fl oz) cold water

Filling:

200g (7oz) prunes

70g (2½oz) unsalted butter

100g (3½oz) caster (superfine) sugar

2 eggs + egg white left from the pastry

180g (6oz) ground almonds

20g (¾oz) plain (all-purpose) flour

1 tsp baking powder

1 tsp almond extract

40g (1½oz) finely grated sweet potato

30g (1oz) chia seeds

40ml (1½fl oz) dark rum

Topping:

50g (2oz) icing (confectioners') sugar

1 tsp almond extract

Cold water, to thin

20g (¾oz) flaked (slivered) almonds

In a large mixing bowl, rub together the first five pastry ingredients until they resemble breadcrumbs. Crack the egg, save the egg white for the filling, and stir in the egg yolk and water and bring together to form a soft dough. Wrap this in cling film, then chill in the fridge for 1 hour.

Preheat the oven to 170°C fan (190°C/375°F/gas mark 5).

Roll out the pastry on a lightly floured surface until it is 5mm (¼in) thick and press this into a 25cm (10in) tart tin. Remember to leave an overhanging collar of pastry around the edge as the pastry will shrink in the oven. Line the pastry case with greaseproof paper and ceramic beans, then bake for 15 minutes. Remove the ceramic beans and bake for another 5 minutes.

While the pastry is baking, soak the prunes in 200ml (7fl oz) boiling water.

Remove the pastry case from the oven and while still warm trim the excess pastry around the edge.

Lower the oven temperature to 150°C fan (170°C/325°F/gas mark 3).

In a mixing bowl, cream together the butter and sugar then beat in 1 egg. Mix in the ground almonds, flour, baking powder, almond extract, then beat in the final egg and egg white. Stir through the sweet potato.

Drain the soaked prunes (retaining the soaking liquid) and blitz half with the chia seeds and the rum using a hand blender until smooth. Spread this over the base of the pastry case. Chop up the remaining prunes and stir through the almond mixture before spooning this into the pastry shell and smooth out. Bake for 40–45 minutes until the frangipane is just firm to touch.

Finally, mix together the icing (confectioners') sugar, the almond extract and just enough water to make a thick icing. Pipe this over the tart in whichever design you like once it is cool, then sprinkle with the almonds.

Prunes

*I want to talk to you about prunes. Wait, come back!
Hear me out . . . We all know that prunes are good for easing
constipation and are particularly popular among people of a certain age.
But although there's nothing I like talking about more than toilet habits,
there's more to prunes than their ability to, let's say, ease one's passage.*

*Prunes are dried plums. Technically, any kind of plum can be processed
into prunes, but some say that damson plums, with their low water
content and thin skin, are best. I grew up in rural Yorkshire, in a house
far too small for our family of seven, but my parents were loath to move
because we had such a huge garden. At the bottom of the jungle-like
orchard, we had a small forest of damson trees, the fruits of which found
their way into many a crumble (although we never had time to pit the
damsons first). Nowadays, my hipster fantasy is to have a garden with
even one damson tree – and, rather than making crumbles, I'd dry the
entire harvest into prunes!*

It's an image thing

Isn't it strange that we find a punnet of plump, ripe plums attractive but turn our noses up at prunes? I mean, what's not to like about a plum that's had its sweet flavour condensed down into one sticky, delicious mouthful?

In the early 2000s, American growers renamed prunes as 'dried plums' in an attempt to rehabilitate their image (complete with pictures of enticing plums on the packaging). But I rather like the word 'prune'. The genus of fruit trees that includes plums is called Prunus (the same family also includes cherries, peaches, nectarines and apricots). And in gardening, to prune is to remove excess growth so a plant can grow more healthily.

Which brings me to the many health benefits of eating prunes. For centuries, prunes were given to sailors at sea to boost the nutrients in their poor diet. Long before that, Roman and Greek doctors used prunes to cure a range of ills.

Prunes are full of insoluble fibre, which as well as keeping you regular, provides food for gut-friendly bacteria and helps to keep your colon healthy.

How to use this hero ingredient

To eat raw, Agen prunes from France are considered the best. (The French love prunes and give them the devotion they deserve.) For cooking and baking, it doesn't really matter what kind of prunes you use, so long as they're moist, sticky and inky-looking. Prunes bring a well-rounded sweetness to recipes, like molasses, but with a sharper, more interesting edge.

You'll find prunes in my:

- Boozy Bakewell tart (see page 231)
- Sticky malt loaf (see page 212)
- Classic fig rolls (see page 198)
- Dark choc energy balls (see page 208)
- Vegan coffee layer cake (see page 186)
- Beet burgers and sweet tato buns (see page 168)

Rice pudding was one of my favourite desserts made by my nana. She made the traditional baked rice pudding that had a thick skin. I loved the skin and the bits of rice at the edge that were like a crust, not because of their texture, but for their flavour. By using toasted rice and coconut you get an almost popcorn flavour, which works really well with bay. Creamy rice pudding only works for me if you have almost equal quantities of fruit to cut through it. The perfumed and caramelly sweetness of a good mango keeps the dessert decadent, yet healthy, and reminds me of a Thai mango sticky rice.

20g (¾oz) jasmine rice

20g (¾oz) desiccated (unsweetened) coconut

1 x 400ml (15fl oz) can coconut milk

100ml (3½fl oz) water

1 tsp malt extract

15g (½oz) caster (superfine) sugar

3 bay leaves

120g (4oz) pudding rice

2 ripe mangoes, peeled, stoned and cut into 1cm (½in) cubes

Toasty rice pudding

In a dry frying pan on a medium heat, toast the jasmine rice, shaking or stirring the pan regularly to ensure each grain is golden brown. Blend the rice in a food processor to a powder.

Back to the dry frying pan, toast the desiccated coconut until fragrant and light brown, then immediately transfer to a bowl and set aside.

Gently heat a saucepan with the coconut milk, water, the malt extract, sugar, bay leaves and rice powder. Add the pudding rice and bring to a simmer, then put on a tight-fitting lid and leave on the lowest heat for 30 minutes without stirring.

To serve, spoon the rice pudding into a glass/bowl, top with the mango and sprinkle with the toasted coconut.

Pickles, ferments and jarred goodness

*the gut feeling
is positive*

We're learning more and more about the health benefits of eating fermented foods, which are produced by micro-organisms (like bacteria or yeast) breaking down the carbohydrates in food and turning them into acids or alcohol. Fermented foods are rich in probiotic bacteria, the good bacteria that are crucial for a healthy gut. So, by eating sauerkraut, live yogurt or (one of my favourites) kimchi, you're feeding your body with live micro-organisms that improve your overall intestinal flora, aid your digestion and boost your immune system.

This age-old process of fermentation is used to preserve foods – or in the case of wine and chocolate (probably two of the most popular fermented goods on the planet), to create something extraordinary from otherwise ordinary ingredients. In other words, as well as boosting shelf life, fermentation also enhances flavour. Pickles and chutneys (which are generally made using vinegar, another fermented food) can also give you a dose of healthy probiotic bacteria, as well as bring a new flavour dimension and texture to foods.

What's great about fermenting, pickling and preserving is it's really easy to do at home. I love playing around with preserving foods, and it's a rare week when we don't have a big jar of home-made kimchi in the fridge. But it's not just about vegetables. You can ferment or pickle grains, like buckwheat or rice, plus citrus fruits, garlic, and even fish. My favourite topping for a stir-fry is pickled mustard leaves. And the Chao (fermented tofu) recipe on page 244 is a must-try.

In Bulgaria, which I try to visit at least once a year, every traditional meal starts with a bowl of pickled vegetables on the table, with forks for everyone (all washed down with a glass of rakia, the local fruit brandy). You don't have to start your dinners in the same way, but I do find the best chutneys, pickles and fermented foods are the ones you can eat alongside lots of different meals. In other words, you might want to expand your collection of jarred goodies beyond the ubiquitous chutney that goes in a cheese sandwich once every six months, or jars that only come out at Christmas.

For example, I use my Tangy carrot chutney (see page 241) with just about anything. And our kimchi jar makes an appearance with many of our main meals (we dip into the jar with chopsticks). The Chao (see page 244) can be mashed up and used to flavour a range of different sauces and meals – use it where you might use soy sauce – and it can even work as a cheese substitute if you don't eat dairy. And my hot chillies (see page 245) are borderline addictive.

Whether you get into fermenting, pickling, making chutneys, or all of the above, you'll soon realise there aren't enough jars in the world, and never enough cupboard space! You have been warned . . .

Making big batches of pickles with a high concentration of vinegar that can be stored for months ensures you have a fantastic stock whenever you want them. I'm not always so organised, however, so with this recipe you'll have pickles ready for the next day. Fermented pickles produce probiotic bacterias in the fermentation process, but even quick pickles provide probiotics through the vinegar used. I use cheap vinegar for cleaning, but it is always good to buy good-quality vinegar for pickling. Most crunchy vegetables work for this recipe, and you can experiment with beetroot, cabbage, unripe melon, unripe mango, turnip or daikon, but my favourite is always cucumber or carrots.

3 medium carrots

3–4 small cucumbers

3 tsp salt

200ml (7fl oz) rice
  wine vinegar

150ml (5fl oz) water

4 tbsp caster (superfine) sugar

3 tbsp white (or yellow)
  mustard seeds

1 garlic clove

1 thumb of fresh root
  ginger, grated

Quick crunchy pickles

Peel and julienne the carrots (or slice into rounds) and slice the cucumbers. Put in a bowl, toss with the salt and leave for 45 minutes. Rinse off the salt and leave to drain in a colander.

Gently heat the vinegar, water, sugar, mustard seeds, garlic and ginger in a small saucepan until the sugar has just dissolved. Allow to cool completely.

Put the carrots and cucumbers in a 1-litre (34fl oz) sterilised jar, pour over the pickling liquor, seal, and put in the fridge.

The pickles are ready the next day and should be eaten within 2 weeks.

I am no kimchi expert, but I am addicted to the stuff. Kimchi is a term for salted and fermented vegetables, but the Chinese cabbage is certainly the most well-known ingredient. Kimchi has grown in popularity because it is delicious, but also for its probiotic benefits. The fermentation process is abundant with an array of different lactic-acid bacteria. If you are looking for probiotic diversity, kimchi delivers. When starting out on your kimchi journey you may want to eat it early in its fermentation, and as you get more tolerant of the tang you can let it develop further. Kimchi is all about experimentation with flavours and the fruits and vegetables. I had the most amazing cauliflower kimchi at a Korean market that I have tried to recreate, but the vendor was not going to betray their secret recipe.

makes 2 x 750ml (26fl oz) jars

1 Chinese cabbage

140g (5oz) salt

1 Korean pear (or an unripe Conference pear), peeled, cored and cut into batons

1 medium carrot, coarsely grated

100g (3½oz) gochujang paste

2 tsp shrimp paste

20ml (¾fl oz) fish sauce

30ml (1fl oz) rice vinegar

5 garlic cloves, minced

Kimchi

Cut the cabbage into quarters and remove the thick inner part to release the leaves.

Dissolve 70g (2½oz) of salt in 500ml (16fl oz) cold water in a large mixing bowl. Push the cabbage leaves into the water and make sure all have been coated. Next, sprinkle the rest of the salt over the leaves, cover, then leave overnight.

In the morning, rinse the leaves well in cold water.

Rinse the large mixing bowl, then cut the cabbage into pieces 2cm x 3cm (¾in x 11/4in) and add to the bowl. Add the pear batons and grated carrot.

In a small bowl, mix the gochujang paste, shrimp paste, fish sauce, rice vinegar and garlic until combined with 60ml (2fl oz) water. Stir this through the vegetables and pear.

Push the vegetables down into 2 jars and leave for 1–2 days outside the fridge – you'll need to leave the jars open at this stage and put something on top of the vegetables to weigh them down (I use a smaller jar filled with water). This ensures any air/gases are released. I periodically press down on the weight at this time, too, to help release the gas further.

Then put the lid on tightly and place in the fridge. You eat the kimchi after 1 week, but I recommend waiting 2 weeks for the flavour to develop.

(See image on page 243.)

Chutneys are a great way to enhance a dish. Growing up I only ever saw chutneys in sandwiches, dolloped alongside a ploughman's salad, or the ubiquitous mango chutney brought out with every curry. I like this recipe as the carrots have a natural sweetness and therefore don't need a lot of extra sugar. I love methodically chopping veg for a chutney, but this one is really quick as the carrots are coarsely grated. Jars of chutney are great to give as gifts, but you need to start hoarding empty jars if you really want to make a hobby of this. Obviously this matches well with cheese, but chutneys are so much more than a friend of cheese and can be an addition to so many meals. I pick at it with chopsticks as I'm eating a stir-fry, add it to tortilla wraps, nestle a dollop next to my salad for work and alongside most curries. Try it, and it will soon become as ubiquitous as tomato ketchup.

300g (10oz) carrots, peeled and coarsely grated

1 small onion, finely chopped

2 garlic cloves, minced

150ml (5fl oz) cider vinegar

150ml (5fl oz) water

110g (4oz) soft brown sugar

2 tsp nigella (black onion) seeds

4 bay leaves

3g salt

Tangy carrot chutney

Add the carrots to a pan with the onion and garlic, then add all the other ingredients. Bring to the boil and simmer vigorously for 5 minutes.

Reduce the heat to a gentle simmer and cook for 45–50 minutes until thickened. You'll need to periodically stir to avoid it sticking to the bottom of the pan.

While the chutney is simmering you'll need to sterilise your jars. Preheat the oven to 160°C fan (180°C/350°F/gas mark 4), wash the jars as normal and place on a baking tray. Once the oven is at temperature, put the jars in for 15 minutes.

Fill the hot jars to the top with the chutney, fit the lids on tightly, then store for at least a month before eating. Store in the fridge once opened and use within 1 month.

(See image on page 242.)

Opposite pickles & ferments.
Top shelf, from left to right: Chao (see page 244),
Lyuti Chusnki (see page 245).
Middle shelf, from left to right: Tangy carrot
chutney (see page 241), Kimchi (see page 240),
Quick crunchy pickles (see page 239).
Above: Kimchi (see page 240).

Fermented tofu ranges in flavour much like the ripeness of cheese. After a couple of weeks it's tangy and soft, and when left for months it goes paste-like and rich. If you're someone that loves the tang of fermented foods you'll love crumbling this into soups or adding it to salad dressings. It is very easy to make, the main thing is to ensure everything is clean and that you have a good supply of jars.

400g (14oz) extra-firm tofu

180ml (6fl oz) water

1 tsp fine salt

1 tsp caster sugar

70ml (2½fl oz) vodka

10ml (¼fl oz) sriracha or
1 tsp gochugaru chilli flakes

Chao (fermented tofu)

Wash your hands well.

Clean your chopping board and knife, then cut the tofu into 1cm (½in) pieces and place on a baking tray lined with kitchen paper. Cover with another layer of kitchen paper and place a baking tray on top. Put a bag of flour on top and leave for 48 hours. It should now smell tangy and may have little white/yellow moulds over it.

Mix all the other ingredients together in a jug to make the brine.

Place the tofu pieces into clean jars and cover with the brine. Secure with a lid (if it's a metal lid, cover with some waxed paper first to avoid the metal reacting with the brine). Keep in a warm place for 3–4 days, then in the fridge for a further week, after which you can eat this, but you can also leave to ferment for longer if you want a really funky flavour. Store in the fridge once opened and use within 1 month.

(See image on page 242.)

I fell in love with these pickled chillies in Bulgaria. They are crunchy, crisp, sweet and sour and, of course, spicy. It is important to salt the chillies overnight to keep them crisp, then allow the pickling liquor to cool before pouring over, as the heat will soften them. I will eat these chillies with most meals, and they're particularly great chopped on top of a salad or pizza. I tend to nibble the crisp flesh and leave the fiery seedy middle.

250g (9oz) jalapeño or serrano chillies

3 tsp salt

Pickling liquor:

160ml (5fl oz) cider vinegar

60ml (2fl oz) water

60g (2oz) caster (superfine) sugar

1 tsp salt

3 garlic cloves, thinly sliced

4 bay leaves

1 tsp black peppercorns

Lyuti Chusnki (Bulgarian pickled chillies)

Take each chilli and prick it three times with a sharp, fine knife just around the crown of the stalk. Put these into a bowl, sprinkle with the salt then leave overnight.

The next day, wash off the salt and pat dry with a clean tea towel or kitchen paper. Pack the chillies into a clean jar.

Put all the ingredients for the pickling liquor into a small saucepan and simmer very gently on a medium heat for 5 minutes.

Allow the liquor to cool before pouring over the chillies and sealing the jar.

Leave for 2–3 weeks to ensure you get a good flavour. Store in a cool, dark place and eat within 1 year. Once opened, store in the fridge.

(See image on page 242.)

About David

David Atherton is a food writer and the winner of *The Great British Bake Off* 2019. On the show, he impressed the judges and public with his interesting flavour combinations, the healthy elements to his bakes and his cool, calm and collected approach in the kitchen.

David grew up in the rural Yorkshire coastal town of Whitby and has been influenced by the food history of this area. His family still lives there and David likes to visit whenever he can and sample the local dishes (and his mum's baking).

For more than a decade David has worked in the international health arena as a global health adviser. His work has taken him around the world from Malawi to Papua New Guinea, and Ethiopia to Myanmar. Wherever he travels he makes sure he experiences as much of the food culture as possible. He has a masters' degree in public health, a post-graduate qualification in expedition and wilderness medicine, and has taught at major universities on HIV and malaria.

David is committed to healthy eating for all ages and has published a children's cookery book and well as writing a Fit Food column for the *Guardian*.

As well as food, David loves fitness (the weekend before *Bake Off* started when everyone was practising their bakes David cycled to Paris). He believes, like food, exercise should be fun and sustainable as part of a healthy lifestyle.

Instagram: @nomadbakerdavid

Twitter: @nomadbakerdavid

Good to Eat

Resources

While the majority of ingredients featured in this book will be available while you do your regular weekly shop, there may be ingredients that you have not heard of, or not seen while browsing the aisle, or tapping through on your online food shop.

Grains, flours and extracts all keep very well, so it is worth making the effort to source and store them. I live in London which has a surfeit of diverse and bountiful food shops. I love taking a trip to a specific shop and exploring their stock – health food shops often have new and interesting grains, but nowadays you can find whatever you want on the internet. You'll still find me wandering around my local Japanese shop, and I always come home with a new ingredient to try along with my white miso.

If you are buying extracts or oils, it is worth making sure you go for good quality. You can use the best main ingredients, and a cheap essence or below par extract is going to make it taste cheap. Conversely, a good-quality extract rich with bountiful compounds will lift even the humblest of main ingredients and make a simple bake sumptuous. Aroma panettone oil from BakeryBits is a favourite citrus oil of mine, and their Amaretto di Saronno Lazzaroni almond extract is the best I've tasted.

My go-to for all things bread is BakeryBits. They have a fabulous website packed with all the equipment and ingredients you'd ever need (and more besides). Organic flours are best to use for sourdough as non-organic varieties often contain chemicals that can harm your starter's micro-organism diversity. I love using Doves farm and Shipton Mill, but there are so many great flours out there, or you could even grind your own.

When it comes to storage, I favour jars. They're non-reactive, easy to clean, and look damn pretty bustling your pantry shelves. One of my biggest kitchen dislikes is when you open a bag of seeds that you hastily sealed with a sticky tab and the packet splits and seeds go everywhere.

When I was on *The Great British Bake Off,* SousChef always came to my rescue. If you're looking for a slightly obscure ingredient, they will almost certainly stock it.

Acknowledgements

This book has been a long time in the making, and is essentially a food journey I have been on since childhood, celebrating the food I eat today. Writing a book is a huge team effort and this book wouldn't be here without the following people:

First and foremost, my mum, who gave me a love for food and inspired me to create, explore and work hard. My partner Nik has not only worked alongside and supported me, he has taught me to love myself and lean into vulnerability, which has enabled me to throw myself into this project. And Kimberley who has been alongside me on my food journey and generously gifted me her recipes, and trained me in her food secrets.

Felicity has represented me better than I can represent myself. I feel privileged to have such a good literary agent and Felicity along with Rosie certainly keep me on track.

The team at Hodder have been incredible and made the process magical. Nicky and Issy have led and listened from the start, and the shoot team Ant, Abi, Natalie, Issy, Flick and Flossy were a dream team!

I feel so privileged to have received the warmth and excitement from mine and Nik's family throughout this project. My twin brother Paul has always been my foodie twin too and this book includes our twin tastes.

A huge thanks to my mentor Dan Lepard who inspired so many of these recipes. Rob has been there for all my highs and lows, and expertly guides me through both.

This book wouldn't have come about without *The Great British Bake Off*. Thank you Jenna for selecting me and making sure I accepted a reserve spot (3 phone calls later). The whole experience was an actual dream come true. Thank you also to Lucie Bruckner who has schooled me in so many things, Michelle for sharing her sourdough knowledge, and Helena for the long phone calls as we went through this book writing experience together. Finally thank you Lisa for encouraging me to apply (simply because she wanted to go to the garden party).

A big shout out all the way to rural Bulgaria to Claire Rustom for helping me with my writing and my voice, Nina for bouncing ideas around for titles, and Herman & Regie for all the support, encouragement and Filipino recipes.

Wow, writing this I am realising how many people it takes to produce a book, and how blessed I am to be surrounded by so many supportive people.

Finally I'd like to thank food, for sustaining me and being the source of my passion.

First published in Great Britain in 2021 by Hodder & Stoughton
An Hachette UK company

1

A CIP catalogue record for this title is available from the British Library

Hardback ISBN 9781529352634
eBook ISBN 9781529352641

Editorial Director: Nicky Ross
Project Editor: Isabel Gonzalez-Prendergast
Editorial Assistant: Olivia Nightingall
Design and Art Direction: Hart Studio
Photography: Ant Duncan
Food Stylist: Natalie Thomson
Props Stylist: Rebecca Newport
Production Manager: Claudette Morris

Colour origination by Alta London
Printed and bound in Germany by Mohn Media GmbH

Hodder & Stoughton policy is to use papers that are natural, renewable and recyclable products and made from wood grown in sustainable forests. The logging and manufacturing processes are expected to conform to the environmental regulations of the country of origin.

Hodder & Stoughton Ltd
Carmelite House
50 Victoria Embankment
London
EC4Y 0DZ
www.hodder.co.uk

Note: All eggs are medium unless otherwise stated.